SPHERE COLOUR PLANT GUIDES
GARDEN PLANTS

D0551070

SPHERE

SPHERE BOOKS LIMITED
30-32 Gray's Inn Road, London WCIX 8JL

CONTENTS

Production: Inmerc BV, Wormer, Holland, and Mercurius
Horticultural Printers, 11 East Stockwell Street, Colchester,
Essex.
Compilation: Rob van Maanen.
Text: A. van Wieringen, Rob van Maanen.
Photography: Joop Valk, Bob van der Lans.
Photo cover: Bob van der Lans.
Layout: Loek de Leeuw.
Lithography: RCO, Velp.
Printing: BV Kunstdrukkerij Mercurius-Wormerveer, Holland.
This edition published by Sphere Books Ltd., London, 1983.
© 1983 Mercbook International Ltd., Guernsey.

INTRODUCTION

Nearly everyone who has a piece of ground by his house tries to make something attractive from it. Only when there is absolutely no other choice is the ground concreted over to make a parking space for the car – and even then there is usually a small strip of grass down the middle.

Plants and flowers create a friendly atmosphere: a house with a garden around it affects you in a different way to a house where nature is missing. And we have not yet mentioned the pleasure of a sunny summer day in the midst of the colour and perfume of a flowery garden.

Dozing in the sun goes with the colour of a flower, the smell of earth and nectar and the hum of insects. But, enough dreaming...

What sort of garden do you have? How would you like it to look? Where is it: in town or country? How big is it, what sort of soil does it have, how many hours of sun does it get each day? How much time can you spare for it? All these questions define what you can do with your garden. If you already know the answers, you can use this guide to gain ideas for enlarging or altering your garden. It offers a wide and varied assortment with – in case it is new to you – the most important information about the plant and its care under each photograph. However, if you do not yet know the answers to the above ques-

tions, then read the following pages before you use the guide.

What exactly is a garden?

A garden is a piece of cultivated landscape. That is to say, a landscape arranged by human hand. It is not, however, a park or meadow – both of which are also part of the cultivated landscape – but a smaller piece of ground with mainly decorative plants. Even so, to differentiate is often difficult: what about a garden of mostly trees and shrubs; or a heather garden which may look as if it came straight from the hills of Scotland; or a natural garden where human hand – for various reasons – has decided to hold back?

It is not the intention here to go into basic theory about the garden, but it is perhaps worth asking yourself what turns a piece of ground into a garden for you? Perhaps one of the following gardens corresponds with your idea and you can make your choice of plants accordingly.

When thinking of a garden many people probably see flowerbeds or borders. That is, a lawn with flowerbeds along its edges. But is there room on 15 square meters of ground for a border?

Yes! In fact it does not matter how small your garden is: even with 4 square meters you can lay a lawn with a number of groups of perennials around it, and in between you can, for

The classical type of garden, the border, consists of a lawn with a strip of plants along its edges.
In this type of garden we mainly find perennials and annuals with a few shrubs or conifers. If the flowering time of the different plants is well combined, the garden will offer a colourful sight from early spring till late autumn.
The lawn provides space for playing, sunbathing and ...mowing!

example, plant bulbs.
Or would you rather have no lawn? Would you prefer to use all the available space to create a garden that flowers for as long as possible? Then take into account the flowering periods of the plants you choose, the shape and colour of the flowers, and how well these colours mix.
Over the years, nurserymen have developed an enormous variety of seeds and plants with lovely flowers. But over the last ten years things have changed.
Gradually rock, heather and natural gardens have gained in popularity and nurseries have adjusted their stocks accordingly. The result is that alongside cultivated plants, nurseries now carry wild

If the soil of your garden is sandy, you might consider the possibility to turn this apparent disadvantage into an advantage; by creating a rockery you will have an 'easy' garden with many possible variations in colour and plant size ...many more than one generally assumes.

plants.

We no longer find just the cultivated plants in a garden, but also those that grow in the wild in this country. This greatly increases the possibilities for your garden.

But remember one thing: your garden only becomes how you want it through the care you give it, and this holds true whether you want flower borders or a natural garden. Obviously some plants need more attention than others, but they all need looking after!

What are your possibilities?
By now you might have some impression of the kind of garden you would like. But there is another question: can you create such a garden? A garden with flowers needs sun..., your sandy earth will never become good garden soil on its own..., you cannot just take a month for a summer holiday without your lawn going brown in the sun – and this happens even in rainy Britain unless you spray it regularly. To help you make a sensible choice – one which allows for the situation in your garden – we must look at what each plant needs from its surroundings. First of all there is the soil in which the plants stand, and which supplies food, water and oxygen. If you want to plant shrubs or conifers in your garden, the earth must be heavy enough to hold the roots firmly; only then will the plant remain upright during a storm. Besides this function, the earth also provides the goodness needed by a plant. The plant takes food from the soil through the threadlike ends of the roots. To transport this food, water is necessary, which the plant also takes from the earth. In addition, moisture is necessary to keep the plant cool in hot weather. Finally, the earth provides the

The past years have shown a growing interest in gardens which contain 'wild' plants. This does not necessarily mean that the plants really are wild. One can however bring out the charm of less cultivated plants by careful choice. But don't be mistaken: this type of garden demands just as much care as any other!

plant with oxygen so that the roots can breathe.
The soil is therefore of vital importance for the plant in several ways.
One type of soil answers the demands of a plant better than another, and you will need to know if the earth in your garden is good enough to successfully sow or plant. So here is some information about the

For good cooks it might be worthwhile to make use of the garden as a supplier of the fresh 'finesse' of their meal.
Many herbs not only have this function, but are medicinal too and, last but not least, they will render your garden colourful with their flowers.

different types of soil and their good and bad points.
The most common in Britain are: clay, peat, sand and loam. Of the clay soils, the river – and young sea – clays give the best drainage; i.e. they are the most crumbly. Water and oxygen can circulate freely.

These clays are very suitable for the garden, although they must be well fertilised in order to give the plant sufficient food. The other types of clay 'ey earth are too badly drained and too fat to be used as garden soil.
Peat forms a very good soil when lime, sand and manure are added. But this generally very wet soil needs extra attention to drainage.
Sandy soil is usually well drained and rich in lime but poor in goodness; mix with compost or stable manure and in summer fertilise regularly since it does not hold its goodness.
Water well, too, because moisture quickly drains away.
Finally, loam is a granular soil that contains some clay.
The more clay, the harder it is to work, but most loam in this

country is fairly light and contains sufficient goodness. The ideal garden soil is crumbly and loose and contains a varied assortment of foods. In addition the ingredients of soil, air and water are present in more or less equal quantities. No one soil matches this ideal, but every soil can be improved. In most cases you can do this by regularly digging in organic fertiliser; i.e. peat, compost (leaf mould) and farmyard manure.

But if you want to tackle the improvement of your garden soil more thoroughly, you can have a soil analysis done by specialists. On the basis of this analysis, they will tell you precisely what you need to do to improve your soil.

In the explanatory text in this guide we give, where necessary, the type of earth best suited to a plant. If this is not specified, the plant will grow in just about any good earth. A plant does not, however, live just from the soil. For growth and flowering light is needed; light provides the energy which develops the plant. And although this energy is generally necessary for the growth of a plant, there are many plants that will grow in shade but only flower in full sun.

So you must bear this in mind when planting out your garden. There are, it is true, some plants that flower in shade, but most, particularly those from seed, only flower with at least two hours of sun per day. Where a plant has a definite preference for sun or shade, you will find this in the text.

If soil and sun are important considerations when choosing where to plant, then so is moisture. If you live on low ground, the soil will generally be damper; peat is often soggy, so good drainage is necessary to ensure the plants survive.

On the other hand, we have established that sandy soil with its crumbly structure does not hold water: even in low lying areas, the ground can be just 10 cm above water level and still be dry. So with sandy soil regular watering is imperative to keep your plants alive. For peat and for sand, the advice is the same: mix the earth with leaf mould and, respectively, sand or peat mould in order to create a consistency that gives good drainage or water retention. Alternatively, you can also select your plants according to soil type. If the earth is sandy you can choose, for example, a rock or heather garden. If you live on damp ground, then consider a garden of reeds and water plants. In most cases, though, and certainly if you live in a town, the situation is not this extreme and you can, with some thought, create a garden in which the different varieties of plants all feel at home.

Now that we have told you something about the demands a plant makes on its surround-

It is possible to make use of a wet soil by turning part of your garden into a water garden. Along the edge of the water you place the plants which like soppy soil. In the pond some of the many types of water plant can find their place.
This type of garden can very well be combined with the garden with wild plants.

ings, we would just like to go into the purpose of this guide. It can help you with ideas for designing or altering your garden. For that reason we have chosen to illustrate as wide a selection of plants as possible. This means that from many widely known plants just the main varieties are included, while in fact there may be many different types of this one plant. For example, the guide is not meant to provide information about every type of tulip, but about as many different plants as possible. We have therefore selected a number of perennials, seeds, tubers and bulbs and wild plants. Shrubs and conifers are only touched on.
For those who are interested, it may be a comfort to know that a further publication in this series, which will appear autumn 1983, will cover trees, shrubs and conifers in depth. Once you have consulted this guide, spend a day with a nurseryman and take a close look at your choice with him. He will also willingly give you advice. We wish you many pleasant hours in your garden!

These, as the name implies, are plants which last many years. It is true that the plants die off in autumn, but in spring they regrow and flower – as long as the earth is well fertilised – just as fully as the year before.

In fact, the plant becomes bushier each year. Perennials are mainly used for the border, where they can be planted in small groups arranged for colour, height and flowering time. If you put low plants at the front with taller ones behind, you will get an upward sloping line that blooms from bottom to top – a tall plant needs more time to reach the stage of flowering than a shorter one. Perennials are very good for combining with annuals from seed and tubers and bulbs. In this way, you can ensure that your garden flowers for long periods. Before planting dig the ground well and work in some dry farmyard manure; preferably in autumn. Plant in spring. During the summer, make sure the plants get enough water, cut off dead flowers and, where necessary, tie up tall plants. After three or four years dig up the plants, cut out the old core and replant the young, strong part.

ACAENA microphylla
New Zealand Burr

Flowering period: July to August.
Colour: olive green, russet.
Height: about 5 cm.
This plant takes very little goodness from the soil. It flourishes in the sun, but can also be grown in shade. Take cuttings in spring or autumn. Spreads well.

ACHILLEA filipendulina
Yarrow

Flowering period: June to August.
Colour: mustard yellow.
Height: about 100 cm.
Prefers a sunny spot whether in well-drained acid or alkali soil. Take cuttings in spring. Suitable for drying but first powder with alum for colour retention.

ACHILLEA millefolium
Yarrow

Flowering period: July.
Colour: cherry red.
Height: about 60 cm.
Prefers a sunny spot whether in well-drained acid or alkali soil. Take cuttings in spring. Suitable for drying.

ACONITUM napellus
Monkshood

Flowering period: July to
August.
Colour: blue, mauve.
Height: 90-120 cm.
The plant requires partial shade at
first; later a sunny spot, as long as
the soil remains sufficiently moist.
Take cuttings early spring. The
roots are poisonous. Good cut
flower.

AGAPANTHUS orientalis
African Lily

Flowering period: July to
September.
Colour: lilac.
Height: 80-120 cm.
A plant with a beautiful bloom,
which will not survive the winter
unless potted in clay'ey soil in a
large pot, kept away from frosts
and allowed to rest. In summer, it
needs a sunny spot.

ALCHEMILLA mollis
Lady's Mantle

Flowering period: June to
August.
Colour: yellow-green.
Height: 30-45 cm.
The plant thrives in any good
garden soil. Best time to transplant
is autumn or spring. Cuttings can
be taken, or use its seeds for
sowing in spring. Good cut flower.

ALSTROEMERIA aurantiaca
Peruvian Lily

Flowering period: June to
September.
Colour: orange.
Height: 90 cm.
This lily is suitable for a sunny,
south-facing bed with well-
drained sandy soil. Take cuttings
or sow seeds in a cold-tray.
Protect young plants against night
frosts.

ALYSSUM saxatile
Golden Alyssum

Flowering period: April to
May.
Colour: pale yellow clusters.
Height: 30 cm.
Easy to grow. Prune after flowering. Thrives in full sun. Propagate
by cuttings or seed. It is a low,
creeping, herb-like plant which is
very useful for rock gardens.

ANAPHALIS triplinervis
Pearl Everlasting

Flowering period: August to
September.
Colour: white.
Height: 20-25 cm.
The plant grows well in a sunny
spot in ordinary garden or sandy
soil. To propagate from seed, plant
out in autumn or spring. Later,
when the plant is fully grown,
cuttings can be taken.

ANEMONE japonica
Windflower

Flowering period: August to
October.
Colour: crimson.
Height: 60-80 cm.
The anemone needs fertile soil
rich in humus, and a sunny or
partially shaded spot. Take
cuttings in spring. It is advisable
to cover the plants if the winter is
harsh.

ANTHEMIS tinctoria
Ox-Eye Chamomile

Flowering period: July to
August.
Colour: golden yellow.
Height: 30-60 cm.
The plant grows in a dry, sunny
spot in good garden soil.
Propagate from cuttings in spring
or autumn, or from seed. Good cut
flower. The yellow chamomile
looks like the common type but is
more cultivated.

AQUILEGIA hybrida
Columbine

Flowering period: May to
June.
Colour: red, pink, mauve,
white, blue, yellow.
Height: 45-60 cm.
Columbine grows best in slightly
damp garden soil in a lightly
shaded spot. Plant spring or
autumn. Propagate by sowing in
spring or by cuttings. Will not
withstand harsh winters or
excessive moisture.

ARABIS arendsii 'Rosabella'
Rock-Cress

Flowering period: April to
June.
Colour: pink.
Height: 10-30 cm.
Grows well in loose, sandy soil.
Take cuttings in autumn. With-
stands frost but not excessive
moisture. Much used for rock
gardens and walls.

ARUNCUS sylvester
Goat's Beard

Flowering period: June and
July.
Colour: yellow-white.
Height: up to 200 cm.
Grows well near water, or in a
damp, shady spot in good soil,
preferably rich in humus. Good cut
flower. Take cuttings in spring.

ASCLEPIAS tuberosa
Milkweed

Flowering period: July to
August.
Colour: scarlet.
Height: about 60 cm.
Thrives in a sunny spot in slightly
dry soil. Soon becomes bushy.
Propagate by cuttings or seeds.
Cover if frosty. Very fragrant
flowers.

ASPHODELINE lutea
Asphodeline

Flowering period: May to July.
Colour: yellow.
Height: 70 cm.
The plant needs well-drained soil with lime in a sunny spot. Propagate by taking off young shoots and planting them out. Sow from April to June.

ASTER dumosus
Michaelmas Daisy

Flowering period: August to October.
Colour: lilac, pink.
Height: 30-50 cm.
Asters are easy to grow. They multiply quickly so that it is usual to take cuttings in the second year, in spring or autumn. They like a sunny, not too dry spot. Very rewarding garden plants, good cut flower.

ASTER novi-belgii
Michaelmas Daisy

Flowering period: September to October.
Colour: rose red, lilac, blue.
Height: up to 120 cm.
Asters like plenty of room in the sun in rich garden soil that dries out slowly. Take cuttings in spring or autumn. Most asters bush out quite quickly. Good cut flower. Deteriorates after two to three years.

ASTILBE arendsii
Astilbe

Flowering period: June to August.
Colour: white-cream.
Height: 60-100 cm.
Plant in autumn or spring in rich, moist garden soil. They grow well near water but also in a herb garden, in partial shade. Good cut flower. Cover in heavy frost.

ASTILBE chinensis 'Pumila'
Astilbe

Flowering period: June to August.
Colour: pink-lilac.
Height: 30 cm.
Plant in autumn or spring in rich, moist garden soil. They grow well near water but also in a herb garden, in partial shade. Good cut flower and spreading plant.

AUBRIETA
Aubrieta

Flowering period: April to May.
Colour: dark blue, pink, mauve.
Height: 7-15 cm.
Definitely a rock or border plant. They also cover dry edges or walls in luxuriant growth. Plant out in autumn or spring in a sunny space. Cut back after flowering. In June plant cuttings in sandy soil.

BELLIS perennis
Daisy

Flowering period: March to September.
Colour: white, red, pink.
Height: about 15 cm.
Border plant. Sow out May or June and plant out in autumn. The plant flowers most of the summer. Although a perennial, it should be treated as a biennial since after a couple of years the flowers decrease.

BERGENIA cordifolia
Bergenia

Flowering period: March to May.
Colour: pink.
Height: about 30 cm.
Not difficult to cultivate. They grow in any soil in both sun and shade Full sun will make the leaves shine. Plant between July and September. Cuttings can be taken in autumn or spring.

BRUNNERA macrophylla
Brunnera

Flowering period: May to June.
Colour: blue with yellow centre.
Height: 30-45 cm.
Grows in moist garden soil in light shade. Take cuttings in autumn or spring. This is a woodland plant which makes a nice show in a flowerbed.

BUPHTHALMUM salicifolium
Buphthalmum

Flowering period: June to July.
Colour: yellow.
Height: 45-60 cm.
This plant thrives in ordinary garden soil in the full sun. Propagate from cuttings taken in spring, or from seed sown under glass in March for planting out in May.

CALTHA pleniflora
King Cup

Flowering period: April to May.
Colour: golden yellow.
Height: 30 cm.
A pretty marsh plant suitable for sunny water margins. Take cuttings early spring. As a garden plant it can only be grown in moist, humus rich soil.

CAMPANULA carpatica
Bellflower

Flowering period: June to August.
Colour: blue, white.
Height: 15-30 cm.
Grows in most soils which hold their moisture, in sun or partial shade. This is a low variety which forms a lovely carpet of flowers in rock gardens or over walls.

CAMPANULA glomerata
Bellflower

Flowering period: June to
August.
Colour: purple.
Height: 30-60 cm.
The bellflower grows best in good
garden soil in a sunny or partially
shady spot. In March take
cuttings, or sow under glass and
plant out in late summer.

CAMPANULA persicifolia
Bellflower

Flowering period: July to
August.
Colour: sky blue, white.
Height: 30-90 cm.
Suitable for a not too sunny,
moderately damp spot in the
garden. They take little goodness
from the soil. Cuttings taken in
spring should be grown in sandy
soil.

CENTAUREA macrocephala
Cornflower

Flowering period: June to
August.
Colour: yellow.
Height: 60-90 cm.
Good bedding plant. Plant out in
spring or autumn in soil with lime.
Take cuttings in spring. Good cut
flower which can also be used in
dried flower bouquets.

CENTAUREA montana
Cornflower

Flowering period: June to
August.
Colour: dark blue, mauve.
Height: 60 cm.
The cornflower is easy to grow. It
needs light soil which can contain
lime. Split the plants for propaga-
tion in spring. Good cut flower.

CENTRANTHUS ruber
Red Valerian

Flowering period: June to
September.
Colour: red.
Height: 60-90 cm.
The plant needs well-drained soil
and a sunny spot. Plant out in
spring or autumn. Propagate by
sowing in the garden in spring.

CERASTIUM tomentosum
Snow-in-Summer

Flowering period: June to
July.
Colour: white.
Height: about 15 cm.
A fast growing, bushy plant that
must be kept in check. Needs
good, well-drained garden soil in
a sunny spot. Take cuttings in
spring or autumn. Good rock
plant.

CERATOSTIGMA plumbagi-
noides
Ceratostigma
Flowering period: August to
September.
Colour: bright blue.
Height: up to 20 cm.
Suitable for rock gardens or
borders. This pretty plant does
well in sun or partial shade in
sandy soil, and gives a mass of
longlasting flowers.

CHRYSANTHEMUM cocci-
neum
Marguerite
Flowering period: May to
June.
Colour: red, crimson, salmon
pink, white.
Height: 75-100 cm.
Plant out spring or early autumn in
well-drained soil in a sunny spot.
Take cuttings in May, June or July.
Very good cut flower.

CHRYSANTEMUM maximum
**Giant Marguerite or Shasta
Daisy**
Flowering period: July to
August.
Colour: white.
Height: 60-90 cm.
The marguerite or Shasta Daisy
grows in any garden soil. Take
cuttings in autumn or spring.
Good cut flower and outstanding
bedding plant. Eventually fertilise
with stable manure.

COREOPSIS verticillata
Coreopsis

Flowering period: June to
September.
Colour: yellow.
Height: 60 cm.
Grows best in well-drained soil in
a sunny spot. Take cuttings from
the large clumps in autumn. This
strong bedding plant is winter
resistant.

CYNOGLOSSUM nervosum
Hound's Tongue

Flowering period: June to
July
Colour: blue.
Height: 45-60 cm.
Grows best in loamy, well-drained
soil in a sunny spot. Propagate in
spring from cuttings or seeds.
Much used in dried flower
bouquets.

DELPHINIUM consolida
Larkspur

Flowering period: May to
July.
Colour: blue, pale blue, pink.
Height: 150-170 cm.
The delphinium needs well-dug,
fertile, well-drained soil. Propa-
gate in spring from cuttings or
seeds. Fine cut flower.

DIANTHUS caesius
Cheddar Pink

Flowering period: June to
July.
Colour: deep pink.
Height: 20 cm.
This pink has a cushion shaped
growth and a fragrant flower. It
needs well-drained soil and a
sunny spot. Cuttings can be taken.

DIANTHUS caryophyllus
Carnation

Flowering period: June to
August.
Colour: red, pink, violet, pale
yellow.
Height: 40-60 cm.
This carnation needs a sunny spot
and well-drained soil with lime.
Propagation usually takes place by
sowing in seed-boxes in spring,
under glass at a moderate
temperature.

DIANTHUS deltoides
Maiden Pink

Flowering period: May to
July.
Colour: pink, red.
Height: 10-15 cm.
This plant needs soil with lime in a
sunny spot. It is of the type that is
easy to cultivate. Propagate by
sowing in spring.

DICENTRA spectabilis
Bleeding Heart

Flowering period: May to
July.
Colour: red-white.
Height: 60-80 cm.
A perennial that does well in not
too dry soil with humus in partial
shade. The flower is heart-shaped
and appears to be crying.
Propagate by division or from
cuttings.

DICTAMNUS albus
Burning Bush

Flowering period: June to
July.
Colour: white, mauve.
Height: 60-90 cm.
Plant out in spring or autumn in
ordinary garden soil in a sunny,
sheltered spot. Propagate from
cuttings or seeds. Once planted,
do not transplant.

DIGITALIS 'Gloxiniaeflora'
Foxglove

Flowering period: June to
July.
Colour: pink, red, yellow.
Height: 120-140 cm.
Sow outside May or June for
flowering the following year, in
ordinary garden soil in sun or
partial shade. Digitalis is a good
plant for the edges of woods where
it will propagate itself. Cuttings
can be taken from the ends of the
stems.

DIPSACUS sylvestris
Wild Teasel

Flowering period: July to
September.
Colour: lilac.
Height: 110 cm.
This plant needs a mixed soil of
clay and lime in the full sun. Sow
in June. It is a fairly rare wild plant.
Good for dried flower bouquets.

DODECATHEON meadia
Shooting Star

Flowering period: May to
June.
Colour: pink, with bright
yellow stamen.
Height: 30-45 cm.
Needs a moist, partially shaded
spot. Take cuttings in autumn. It is
a good idea to combine it with
other moisture loving plants that
have different flowering periods.

DORONICUM caucasicum
Leopard's Bane

Flowering period: April to
May.
Colour: dark yellow.
Height: 30-40 cm.
Needs slightly moist soil in a
sunny or lightly shaded spot. Take
cuttings from the roots in late
summer. Also suitable for the
darker town garden.

DRYAS suendermannii
Dryas

Flowering period: May to
June.
Colour: white.
Height: 20 cm.
This is a turf-like plant that does
best in a sunny rock garden in soil
with lime. Nurseries sell them as
pot plants which can be planted
out in favourable weather. They
can also be propagated by
splitting the roots.

DUCHÉSNEA indica
Ornamental Strawberry

Flowering period: May to
June.
Colour: yellow; red fruit.
Height: 5-10 cm.
The ornamental strawberry needs
humus rich, moist soil. Propagate
from seed or young shoots. Good
spreading plant, which can also be
used as hanging plant for walls.
The imitation fruit appears from
July.

ERICA darlyensis
Heather

Flowering period: November
to April.
Colour: pink-purple.
Height: up to 50 cm.
Needs a spot in the sun or partial
shade and some lime in the soil.
Immediately after flowering prune
slightly to prevent uneven growth.
Take cuttings in summer.

ERIGERON hybride
Fleabane

Flowering period: June to August.
Colour: shades of pink, lilac, purple, mauve.
Height: 45-60 cm.
Plant out in autumn or early spring in a sunny spot in ordinary soil. Propagate by dividing the root clumps in autumn or spring; by cuttings or seeds. Very good cut flower.

ERODIUM
Stork's Bill

Flowering period: May to August.
Colour: rose red.
Height: 5 cm.
A turf-like plant too delicate for our winters. It can, however, be potted for the winter and kept in a cool place. Needs a sunny spot, in well-drained soil. It is primarily a rock plant.

EUPHORBIA myrsinites
Spurge

Flowering period: May to June.
Colour: cream.
Height: 15 cm.
Grows in relatively poor soil, in a sunny or partially shady spot. Cuttings can be taken. Perennial for use as rock plant.

EUPHORBIA polychroma
Spurge

Flowering period: April to May.
Colour: yellow.
Height: 40-50 cm.
Grows in relatively poor soil, in a sunny or partially shady spot. Cuttings can be taken. Good bedding plant.

FUCHSIA hybride
Fuchsia

Flowering period: July to September.
Colour: red, pink, white, mauve.
Height: 80-100 cm.
The plant needs ordinary garden soil with lime, good drainage, sun or partial shade; in a trough, pot or flowerbed. It will not survive the winter unless potted and kept at 5° Centigrade.

GAILLARDIA grandiflora
Blanket Flower

Flowering period: June to October.
Colour: yellow, red.
Height: 60 cm.
Thrives in a sunny spot in light, well-drained soil. Take cuttings in spring. The plant will not survive too much moisture in winter.

GENTIANA acaulis
Gentian

Flowering period: August to
September.
Colour: deep blue.
Height: 5-10 cm.
The gentian needs a humus rich,
moist soil in a lightly shaded spot.
Propagate in autumn by sowing in
trays or pots.

GERANIUM endressii
Cranesbill

Flowering period: June to
October.
Colour: pale pink.
Height: 20-40 cm.
This plant loves sun and rather
stony soil. It forms large clumps
from which pieces can be lifted in
autumn or spring. Very good
spreading plant.

GERANIUM subcaulescens
Cranesbill

Flowering period: June to
July.
Colour: crimson.
Height: about 15 cm.
This plant needs a sunny spot in a
rock garden. The soil should be
neither too dry nor too damp.
Cuttings can be taken.

GEUM coccineum
Avens

Flowering period: June to
September.
Colour: orange.
Height: 30 cm.
Grows in ordinary garden soil in a
sunny or lightly shaded spot.
Cuttings can be taken. Sow in
March-April in cold-tray. The plant
then flowers the following year

GYPSOPHILA paniculata
Maiden's Breath

Flowering period: May to
August.
Colour: white.
Height: 60-90 cm.
Plant out maiden's breath in
spring in lime rich soil in a sunny
spot. Take cuttings for rooting late
summer. Good cut and dry flower.

HEBE armstrongii
Hebe

Flowering period: July.
Colour: white.
Height: about 50 cm.
This is a delicate plant which looks
like a conifer. It grows best in lime
rich soil. Take cuttings after
flowering. It is a nice plant with
which to fill troughs and pots for
the winter.

HELENIUM
Helenium

Flowering period: July to September.
Colour: yellow with brown.
Height: 60-90 cm.
Grows in all good garden soils, but heavy clay is ideal. Plant out in autumn or spring, and propagate from cuttings or seeds. The masses of young shoots which grow under the plant can also be used.

HELIANTHEMUM
Rock Rose

Flowering period: June to July.
Colour: pink.
Height: about 30 cm.
The rock rose needs a sunny spot in ordinary soil and is ideal for dry walls, rock gardens and terraces. Take cuttings for rooting. Plant in sandy compost July-August. A much loved plant.

HELIANTHUS sparsifolius
Sunflower

Flowering period: August to October.
Colour: golden yellow.
Height: 180-240 cm.
For the best results plant in clay'ey soil in the sun. Fertilise occasionally to promote growth. Take cuttings in autumn. A very good cut flower.

HELIOPSIS scabra
Heliopsis (single)

Flowering period: June to July.
Colour: yellow.
Height: 100-150 cm.
Needs a sunny spot in ordinary garden soil. Take cuttings March-April. Good cut flower. Allow 50 cm between plants. A very strong, winter-proof perennial with a luxuriant, long-lasting bloom.

HELIOPSIS scabra
Heliopsis (double)

Flowering period: June to July.
Colour: yellow.
Height: 100-150 cm.
Needs a sunny spot in ordinary garden soil. Take cuttings March-April. Good cut flower. Allow 50 cm between plants. Use this perennial at the back of the flower bed or in front of a row of shrubs.

HELLEBORUS niger 'Maximus'
Christmas rose
Flowering period: January to February.
Colour: white, rose red.
Height: 40 cm.
Needs well-drained soil and a shady spot. Before planting, mix the soil with a lot of cow dung and leaf mould. Take cuttings in spring, or sow in coldtray if the seeds are ripe.

**HEMEROCALLIS hybride
Day Lily**

Flowering period: July to August.
Colour: pink, yellow, russet, purple.
Height: 60-100 cm.
This lily grows best in ordinary, preferably moist, garden soil, but not beside water; it needs a sunny or lightly shaded spot. Propagate from cuttings or seeds. Cover during heavy frosts.

**HEUCHERA
Coral Flower**

Flowering period: May to August.
Colour: dark or bright red.
Height: 45-60 cm.
Grows in ordinary garden soil in the sun or partial shade. A shovelful of compost in spring promotes growth. Propagate by splitting or seeds. Cover in severe winters.

**HOSTA fortunei
Plantain Lily**

Flowering period: May.
Colour: lilac.
Height: 45-60 cm.
This plant is distinguished by its huge leaves, which often have variegated spots, veins or edges. It grows well in moist garden soil in sun or partial shade; also beside water. Take cuttings in spring.

**HUTCHINSIA alpina
Hutchinsia**

Flowering period: April-May-June.
Colour: white.
Height: 5-10 cm.
Needs little goodness from the soil; but does like sun or slight shade and sufficient moisture during flowering. Cuttings can be taken. Nice rock plant.

**HYPERICUM calycinum
Aaron's Beard**

Flowering period: June to September.
Colour: bright yellow.
Height: 30 cm.
This plant has large yellow blooms, measuring some 7 cm. It grows like a small shrub, along the ground, in good well-drained garden soil, in sun or partial shade. Take cuttings in spring.

**IBERIS sempervirens
Candytuft**

Flowering period: March to May.
Colour: white.
Height: 20-30 cm.
Iberis should be sown several millimeters deep in March or April in light soil (and in August for autumn flowering). Thin out seedlings to 5 cm intervals. Keep soil moist. Take cuttings from the roots.

INCARVILLEA delavayi
Incarvillea

Flowering period: May to June.
Colour: bright rose pink.
Height: 30-45 cm.
A plant that needs a lot of care in our climate. Well dug ground mixed with soft cow dung and leaf mould; and a sheltered, sunny spot. Take cuttings carefully from roots in spring.

INULA orientalis
Inula

Flowering period: July to August.
Colour: yellow.
Height: 75-100 cm.
Needs ordinary garden soil – but not too dry – and a sunny spot. Prune every 3-4 years in spring. Decorative in rock gardens or beds.

IRIS germanica
Iris

Flowering period: May to July.
Colour: lilac, yellow, pink, white, blue.
Height: 60-90 cm.
Suitable for well-drained, moist soil with lime, in a sunny spot. When planting, allow root stock to show just above the soil. Good cut flower.

IRIS kaempferi
Iris

Flowering period: June to July.
Colour: lilac, pink, blue, white.
Height: 60-80 cm.
This type grows in 5 to 10 cm deep water and does well in moist soil or along the edge of a pond. Good cut flower. The soil must have no lime in it, and should preferably be fertile clay.

IRIS pseudacorus
Yellow Flag

Flowering period: May to June.
Colour: bright or orange yellow.
Height: 60-90 cm.
The flag is suitable for moist soils, pond edges or the banks of streams. Best method of propagation is by dividing the roots in spring once the plant is a few years old. Good cut flower.

IRIS sibirica
Iris

Flowering period: June to July.
Colour: white, dark mauve.
Height: 90-120 cm.
A moisture loving plant with strong, spreading roots, that will grow in dryer soil. Needs fertile, clay'ey soil without lime. Like other irises, a good cut flower.

KNIPHOFIA uvarla gr. fl.
Red Hot Poker

Flowering period: July to September.
Colour: coral, later changing to orange.
Height: 80-100 cm.
Plant out in autumn or spring in fertile, well-drained soil. Cover in winter. Take cuttings in spring or autumn. Needs sun. Good cut flower.

LATHYRUS latifolius
Everlasting Pea

Flowering period: June to September.
Colour: white, pink, crimson.
Height: 25-300 cm (climber).
Sow in cold-tray and plant out late March in well-dug and fertilised soil. Or early spring under glass, harden off plants and plant out early May for late bloom. Good cut flower.

LAVANDULA officinalis
Lavender

Flowering period: July to September.
Colour: pale or dark violet, purple.
Height: 40-50 cm.
Plant lavender in loose soil, well dug with compost or old cow dung. Spread the roots well when planting. It has a lovely scent and is often dried and sewn into small bags for use in the linen cupboard.

LAVATERA olbia 'Rosea'
Mallow

Flowering period: June to October.
Colour: rose red.
Height: 150-180 cm.
Needs ordinary garden soil in a sunny spot. Take cuttings in spring, and grow under a cold cloche. Sowing in a cold green-house in spring is also possible. Good cut flower.

LEONTOPODIUM alpinum
Edelweiss

Flowering period: May to July.
Colour: silver outer petals round yellow centre.
Height: 10-20 cm.
Edelweiss is an easy to grow rock plant that needs well drained soil in a sunny spot. Sow in seed-tray in March or April, and later plant out. Might flower the following year. Good for rock gardens.

LIATRIS spicata
Gay Feather

Flowering period: July to September.
Colour: reddish-mauve.
Height: 70-80 cm.
Liatris must have a sunny spot and fairly light soil. Take cuttings in spring; sow in light soil late summer. Good cut flower.

LIGULARIA dentata
Ligularia

Flowering period: July to September.
Colour: orange-yellow.
Height: 90-120 cm.
Grows in damp places or beside water in sun or partial shade. Take cuttings in spring. The plant has pretty leaves and makes a nice decoration for the garden.

LIGULARIA przewalskii
Ligularia

Flowering period: June to August.
Colour: orange.
Height: 120-150 cm.
This prefers well-drained but not too dry soil in sun or partial shade. Take cuttings in spring; this should be in March or April because of the late bloom.

LINUM perenne
Flax

Flowering period: June to August.
Colour: blue.
Height: about 50 cm.
Flax grows in light, well-drained soil in full sun. Propagate by sowing out in spring; or by taking cuttings from the roots in spring. This plant also spreads its own seeds.

LITHOSPERMUM diffusum
Gromwell

Flowering period: May to July.
Colour: bright gentian blue.
Height: 15 cm.
Needs peaty soil and a sunny spot, and does not like lime in the soil. If conditions are right, the plant will spread considerably. Very good for growing over walls.

LOBELIA cardinalis
Lobelia

Flowering period: July to August.
Colour: scarlet.
Height: 90-150 cm.
After planting the lobelia must be well watered as it is originally a riverside plant. It will not survive harsh weather and must be covered in winter. Propagate from cuttings or seeds in March at 10-15°Centigrade.

LUPINUS russell hybride
Lupin

Flowering period: May to June.
Colour: blue, pink, yellow, red.
Height: 80 cm.
The lupin must be cut back every three years as the old plant dies. Needs light, sandy soil in sun or partial shade. Can be planted in spring or autumn. Good cut flower.

LYCHNIS coronaria
Campion

Flowering period: July to
August.
Colour: rose red.
Height: 45-60 cm.
Grows in ordinary, well-drained
garden soil in a sunny spot. Take
cuttings in spring. In addition, the
plant will spread its own seeds.
Primarily a bedding plant.

LYSIMACHIA clethroides
Lysimachia

Flowering period: July to
August.
Colour: white.
Height: 60-80 cm.
Needs fertile soil and thrives
beside water, in sun or partial
shade. Good cut flower. Propagate
by division. Good bedding plant as
long as the soil is sufficiently
moist.

LYSIMACHIA punctata
Lysimachia

Flowering period: May to
July.
Colour: yellow
Height: 90 cm.
The plant prefers fertile soil and
grows well beside water. Can take
the sun or partial shade. Take
cuttings in spring or autumn
Decorative bedding plant.

MALVA alcea
Musk Mallow

Flowering period: July to
October
Colour: pale pink to white.
Height: 90-120 cm.
Grows in ordinary garden soil in a
sunny spot. Propagate by sowing
in spring in cold-trays in sandy
soil. Cuttings can also be taken for
rooting, or it can be left simply to
run wild. Gives longlasting cut
flowers.

MIMULUS 'burnettii'
Monkey Flower

Flowering period: June to
October.
Colour: orange red.
Height: 20-30 cm.
Suitable for sunny or partially
shaded, moist spot. Can be sown
under glass in seedboxes in a light
earth mixture. Young shoots can
be rooted in spring.

MONARDA didyma
Bergamot

Flowering period: June to
August.
Colour: scarlet.
Height: 80-100 cm.
Needs a moist spot in sun or
partial shade. In dry periods keep
soil wet, and put peat dust or
compost around the plant.
Propagate from root cuttings in
spring. A fairly strong, summer
blooming bedding plant.

MYOSOTIS palustris
Water Forget-me-Not

Flowering period: May to June.
Colour: blue with yellow eye.
Height: 15-30 cm.
Sow outside in shallow furrows between April and June. Plant out seedlings in October at 10-15 cm intervals. Take cuttings in March or October.

NEPETA faassenii

Flowering period: May to August.
Colour: lavender blue.
Height: 30-45 cm.
Grows in light soil in a sunny spot. Wilts quickly if soil is too moist. Take cuttings in spring. Root in sandy soil in a cold-frame. Good for growing in a heather garden or as border plant.

OENOTHERA missouriensis
Evening Primrose

Flowering period: July to August.
Colour: lemon yellow.
Height: 15-25 cm.
This plant grows in well-drained soil in sun or partial shade. Propagate from seed. Very good for rock gardens and spreads well.

PAEONIA sinensis
Peony

Flowering period: May to June.
Colour: red.
Height: about 60 cm.
The peony is a favourite bedding plant, suitable for a sunny or partially shaded spot. Before planting, dig and fertilise the soil. It has woody roots and does not transplant well. Take cuttings in autumn. Cover against frosts.

PAPAVER nudicaule
Iceland Poppy

Flowering period: April to August.
Colour: yellow, white, orange.
Height: 35 cm.
Plant in October or early spring in well dug, loamy soil in full sun. Cover with compost in March-April. Take cuttings in March or in winter for rooting.

PAPAVER orientale
Eastern Poppy

Flowering period: late May to June.
Colour: red, orange.
Height: 35-60 cm.
Perennial poppies come in a wide range. We limit ourselves to the 'orientale'. This eastern poppy loves the sun but not too much moisture. Propagate by splitting the roots.

PHLOX paniculata
Phlox

Flowering period: July to September.
Colour: white, pink, purple, red.
Height: about 90 cm.
Phlox must have good garden soil which must not dry out and full sun. Root cuttings in late summer in boxes filled with sand. Plant resulting small plants in summer. Good, sweet smelling cut flower.

PHLOX subulata
Phlox

Flowering period: April to June.
Colour: purple, white.
Height: 10 cm.
This phlox likes fertile soil in the sun in a rock garden or against a wall. Propagate by dividing roots in March. When left to grow freely it is very suitable for troughs, tubs, hanging pots, etc. Good cut flower.

PHYGELIUS capensis
Phygelius

Flowering period: July to September.
Colour: red.
Height: about 75 cm.
Valuable plant for a mild climate. Grows well in full sun and is easy to propagate late summer. Pot for the winter and keep in a cool place away from frosts.

PHYSALIS franchetii
Chinese Lantern

Flowering period: June.
Colour: white, with large, full orange coloured fruit.
Height: 45 cm.
Plant out in spring or autumn in well-drained, clay'ey or loamy soil in sun or partial shade. Take cuttings from roots in spring.

PHYSOSTEGIA virginiana
Obedient Plant

Flowering period: July to September.
Colour: pink, white.
Height: 60-100 cm.
The plant needs sun or partial shade in ordinary garden soil. Plant out in spring. Cuttings can be taken. The flowers can be turned with a finger.

PLATYCODON gr. fl. 'Mariesi'
Balloon Flower

Flowering period: June to September.
Colour: dark purple.
Height: 30-40 cm.
In bud the bloom resembles an inflated balloon. Suitable for sun or partial shade. Sow in cold-frame March-April or outside April-May. Some bloom the same year, others the following year.

POLEMONIUM caeruleum
Jacob's Ladder

Flowering period: May to September.
Colour: blue.
Height: 45-75 cm.
Plant in autumn in ordinary garden soil. Propagate from cuttings or seeds late summer. Can flourish in light shade. Luxuriant blooming, bedding or rock plant.

POLYGONATUM odoratum
Solomon's Seal

Flowering period: May to June.
Colour: white (flower); blue-black (berry).
Height: 30-50 cm.
Often found in woods and dunes; it needs moist soil with humus in partial shade. Propagate by dividing the root stock. A good, long lasting cut flower.

POLYGONUM affine
Knotweed

Flowering period: August to October.
Colour: rose red.
Height: 15-30 cm.
This is a turf-like, tight leafed plant. It needs a lot of sun, and spreads very quickly.

POTENTILLA nepalensis
Cinquefoil

Flowering period: June to September.
Colour: rose red.
Height: 45 cm.
Needs well-drained soil. Fertilise in summer. Plant in a sunny spot. Cuttings can be taken. Good rock plant which spreads well. It is a good idea to rejuvenate the plant by occasional pruning.

POTENTILLA tonguei
Cinquefoil

Flowering period: July to August.
Colour: yellow, orange-red.
Height: 8 cm.
The soil must be well-drained and fertile. It needs sun and fertiliser in summer. Propagate by sowing under glass in March. Plant out seedlings in May or June.

PRIMULA acaulis
Primrose

Flowering period: March to April.
Colour: yellow, white, blue, pink, purple.
Height: 10-15 cm.
Primula needs a cool, sunny or partially shaded spot in peat or leaf mould. Propagate from sideshoots in spring. The blooms are large and velvety.

PRIMULA denticulata
Drumstick Primrose

Flowering period: March to May.
Colour: pale or dark purple, mauve, white, with yellow.
Height: 15-25 cm.
The plant flowers before the leaves appear. Needs moist, light soil in partial shade. Sow In May-June at about 16°Centigrade

PRUNELLA vulgaris
Self-Heal

Flowering period: June to September.
Colour: purple.
Height: 20 cm.
Not a demanding plant, it is low and strong. It prefers a soil rich in lime. Prune and transplant each year. Can also be raised from seed. Good rock or border plant which spreads well.

PULMONARIA saccharata
Lung-wort

Flowering period: April to July.
Colour: pink.
Height: up to 30 cm.
Grows in most soils, in both sun and shade. Propagate from seed sown outside in March or April, or by taking cuttings in the fourth or fifth year.

PULSATILLA vulgaris
Pasque Flower

Flowering period: April.
Colour: pale violet.
Height: 30 cm.
This plant needs a light, open spot, with lime rich soil. Must be protected against frost and molsture In winter. Propagate by sowing in sandy soil in a cold-tray in July or August.

RANUNCULUS lingua
Great Spearwort

Flowering period: June to July.
Colour: yellow.
Height: 90-120 cm.
A giant version of the well known buttercup. A water or bank plant that thrives best in sun or partial shade and, obviously, in moist soil. It is a nice plant for the natural garden, but it spreads like wildfire.

RHEUM palmatum
Ornamental Rhubarb

Flowering period: June.
Colour: cream to dark red.
Height: 150-180 cm.
The plant can be grown in fertile soil. It needs a lot of space due to the large leaves. During growing period it needs a lot of water. Shoots from the main plant can be planted out in March or September-October.

RUDBECKIA nitida
Coneflower

Flowering period: July to September.
Colour: yellow with brown centre.
Height: 200 cm.
Prefers good garden soil and a sunny spot. Take cuttings spring or autumn. A lovely bedding plant which cheers up a garden in late summer and autumn. Good cut flower.

RUDBECKIA purpurea
Coneflower

Flowering period: August to September.
Colour: mauve.
Height: 80 cm.
Plant out in spring or autumn in fertile, well-drained soil in full sun. Take cuttings spring or autumn. Good cut flower, gives masses of blooms and spreads quickly.

SAGINA subulata
Awl-leaved Pearlwort

Flowering period: May to June.
Colour: bright white.
Height: 3-5 cm.
Needs sufficient light but must be protected against strong sunlight. The soil must be sufficiently moist. Sometimes used instead of grass.

SALVIA nemerosa
Salvia

Flowering period: May to September.
Colour: blue.
Height: 40-60 cm.
Salvias are easily grown in ordinary, well-drained garden soil in a sunny spot. Take cuttings in spring. This salvia is a fine bedding plant.

SANTOLINA chamaecyparis-sus
Cotton Lavender
Flowering period: July to August.
Colour: deep yellow.
Height: up to 75 cm.
This must be planted in the sunniest possible spot in poor, sandy soil. It can be easily propagated by rooting cuttings mid or late summer. Look out for frost damage.

SAPONARIA ocymoides
Soapwort

Flowering period: May to July.
Colour: rose red.
Height: 10 cm.
Saponaria needs sun and well-drained, fertile soil. Plant out between April and October. Propagate from cuttings between October and March, or by rooting in a tray in autumn.

SAXIFRAGA aizoon
Saxifrage

Flowering period: June to July.
Colour: cream.
Height: 7-10 cm.
This saxifrage prefers a sunny spot and well-drained ground, although little soil is necessary. Take cuttings late summer. Flourishes in a rock garden.

SAXIFRAGA arendsii
Saxifrage

Flowering period: May.
Colour: pink, red.
Height: about 30 cm.
Cushion shaped plant needing little soil. Likes a sunny, not too moist spot. Good in rock garden or flowerbed.

SCABIOSA caucasica
Scabious

Flowering period: June to October.
Colour: lilac, purple.
Height: 70-80 cm.
The plants grow well in soil with lime that has been well fertilised. Take cuttings every three or four years. Good bedding plant and fine cut flower.

SEDUM acre
Biting Stonecrop

Flowering period: June to August.
Colour: yellow.
Height: 5-10 cm.
Stonecrop grows in dry, sandy soil and is a decorative wall or rock plant which spreads well. Plant out between November and April. Water sparingly in summer. Cuttings can be taken.

SEDUM ewersii
Sedum

Flowering period: July to September.
Colour: purple-pink.
Height: about 5 cm.
Thrives in any well-drained soil. Likes full sun. Can be planted in the driest (highest) spot in the garden. Cuttings can be taken. Very good rock plant.

SEDUM spathulifolium
Sedum

Flowering period: May to June.
Colour: pale yellow; leaf edge is grey-green or pink.
Height: 8-10 cm.
Best time to plant this and the sedum spectabile is spring or autumn. It needs well-drained soil and cuttings can be taken in spring.

SEDUM spectabile
Sedum

Flowering period: July to
September.
Colour: pink with mauve tinge.
Height: up to 60 cm.
Best time to plant is spring or
autumn. The plant has fleshy
leaves. It needs well-drained soil
and cuttings can be taken in
spring.

SEMPERVIVUM
Houseleek

Flowering period: June to
July.
Colour: pink.
Height: 10-20 cm.
Grows best in a sunny spot in a
rock garden. Plant out between
March and June in garden
compost. Propagate by potting the
small rosettes. It is used in the
Alps (on farm roofs) as protection
against lightning.

SEMPERVIVUM arach-
noideum
Cobweb Houseleek
Flowering period: June to
August.
Colour: deep pink, bright red.
Height: 5-15 cm.
Has long, interwoven leaf fibres
which look like cobwebs. Thrives
in a sunny, dry spot; such as a
rocky slope. Take cuttings spring
or autumn.

SIDALCEA hybride
Sidalcea

Flowering period: June to
August.
Colour: lilac.
Height: about 40 cm.
Sidalcea grows in all garden soils,
but a sunny spot is essential. Plant
out in spring or autumn. Take
cuttings every three or four years
in October or March.

SISYRINCHIUM angustifolium
Blue-eyed Grass

Flowering period: June to
July.
Colour: blue.
Height: 20 cm.
Needs well-drained soil in a sunny
spot. Take cuttings in spring. It is a
good idea to do this again every
three years.

SOLIDAGO hybride
Golden Rod

Flowering period: July to
October.
Colour: yellow.
Height: 75-100 cm.
Golden rod needs ordinary garden
soil in the sun. The taller ones
need some support. Take cuttings
in spring or autumn; it is important
to do this every three years.

STACHYS lanata
Lamb's Tongue

Flowering period: July.
Colour: purple.
Height: 30 cm.
Grows well in a sheltered bed in ordinary garden soil. It must be planted in spring or autumn. At the same time it can be propagated by dividing the tuber shaped roots.

THALICTRUM aquilegifolium
Meadow Rue

Flowering period: May to July.
Colour: pale purple, pink.
Height: about 75 cm.
Grows in all not too dry garden soils in sun or partial shade. Sow under glass in seedbox with sandy soil in spring. Old plants can be taken out.

TIARELLA cordifolia
Foam Flower

Flowering period: April to July.
Colour: white.
Height: 15-30 cm.
Needs a slightly shady spot and loose, humus rich soil. The flower does not last long, but the leaf is decorative. Plant out in spring and take cuttings in autumn.

TRADESCANTIA virginiana
Trinity Flower

Flowering period: May to September.
Colour: blue.
Height: 30-50 cm.
Grows in ordinary garden soil in sun or light shade. Take cuttings every 3-4 years in spring or autumn. Very good bedding plant; also grows well beside water.

TROLLIUS hybride
Globe Flower

Flowering period: May to July.
Colour: dark yellow.
Height: 60-80 cm.
Likes to grow by a pond. Plant early spring in partial shade or full sun. Soil should be well dug and moist. Take cuttings third or fourth year in autumn. Good cut flower.

VERBASCUM hybride
Mullein

Flowering period: June to August.
Colour: yellow.
Height: up to 90 cm.
A very decorative plant that grows in well-drained soil with lime. After several years the plant usually dies. Prior to this propagate from seed or cuttings in spring or autumn.

VERONICA spicata
Spiked Speedwell

Flowering period: June to August.
Colour: bright blue.
Height: 30-60 cm.
Speedwell grows in ordinary soil in a sunny spot. Plant out and take cuttings in spring or autumn. Looks very nice in a natural garden, but also in a cultivated bed.

VINCA minor
Lesser Periwinkle

Flowering period: April to September.
Colour: blue.
Height: 15 cm.
Because of its long shoots, this plant forms a good soil covering. Does well in both sun and shade. Cut back in early spring and propagate from the cuttings.

VIOLA cornuta
Pansy

Flowering period: June to August.
Colour: violet.
Height: 10-30 cm.
Pansies grow well in moist, well-drained soil in partial shade. Propagate from cuttings which should be rooted in a cold-frame in sandy soil.

VIOLA odorata
Sweet Violet

Flowering period: March.
Colour: purple or white.
Height: about 10 cm.
A winter resistant perennial. The soil must be fertile and well-drained. Plant the clumps in April or September in a sheltered spot. Propagate from the ground shoots in April.

WALDSTEINIA ternata
Waldsteinia

Flowering period: April to May.
Colour: yellow.
Height: 7-10 cm.
A rock plant which grows in ordinary, well-drained soil in a cool spot. Take cuttings in autumn. This type has a tendency to run wild.

YUCCA filamentosa
Adam's Needle

Flowering period: July to October.
Colour: white.
Height: 120-450 cm.
Must be planted in a warm spot in full sun. It is a decorative plant. Make sure the soil is well dug and fertilised. Protect against frost and moisture in winter.

These are the plants which give your garden most of its colour. With their bright hues and richness of bloom, they can be put between perennials, along edges or in tubs, and will adorn your garden for months. Plants from seed usually last one or two years, but there are some which will last longer. Perennials and bulbs and tubers from seed are not generally included under this heading.

These plants are much used along edges and in tubs and, because they bloom well, in open spaces in the flowerbed.

In general they make few demands and offer inexhaustible possibilities for changing your garden every year.

Annuals from seed are normally sown under glass in February-March (for early flowering), or in April-May outside. Biennials from seed are sown out in summer; and need the winter to build up their strength for their early flowering period. Seed is sown in rows or just scattered, in a seedbed or the final planned spot. When the seedlings appear they can be thinned out, making more room for growth.

ACROLINEUM helipterum roseum
Acrolineum
Flowering period: 6 to 8 weeks between July and September.
Colour: red, white, pink.
Height: up to 60 cm.
Sow under glass in April. Plant out mid-May at 20 cm intervals. Or sow outdoors from early May and thin out later. Fairly rich, loose soil; sunny spot. Beautiful drying flower.

ADONIS aestivalis
Pheasant's Eye

Flowering period: a few weeks between June and August.
Colour: red.
Height: up to 40 cm.
Sow in April or May. The small flowers are beautiful and the plant demands little attention, but the flowering period is fairly short.

AGERATUM mexicanum
Ageratum

Flowering period: July to October.
Colour: blue, mauve, pink, white.
Height: 10-25 cm.
Sow under glass between February and April. Plant out end of May at 20 cm intervals. Prefers a sunny spot. Good for use as border plant.

ALTHAEA rosea
Hollyhock

Flowering period: July to September.
Colour: pink, crimson, yellow, white.
Height: 1¹/₂-2¹/₂ m.
Sow on chosen spot in the autumn and thin out in the spring. Hollyhocks need a sunny place, well-drained soil and support for their height and the weight of their large flowers.

ALYSSUM lobularia maritima
Sweet Allison

Flowering period: June to October.
Colour: white.
Height: 10 cm.
Sow under glass in March and plant out in May, or sow outdoors in April or May and thin out to 20 cm intervals. This low plant is primarily a rock plant, but also comes into its own along the border of a flower bed.

AMARANTHUS caudatus
Amaranthus, Love-lies-bleeding
Flowering period: July to September.
Colour: mauve-red.
Height: 60-100 cm.
Sow in March, April or May in a seedbed or on the chosen spot. Thin out to a relative distance of 40 cm. The plant is difficult to combine with other garden plants, but the long plumes are ideal for flower arrangements.

ANAGALLIS arvensis
Scarlet Pimpernel

Flowering period: May to October.
Colour: mauve, red, pink.
Height: 20 cm.
Sow outside in April-May and slightly thin out, or under glass in March for planting out in May. The plant lends itself well to filling in between other annual summer flowers and for rock gardens.

ANTIRRHINUM majus maximum
Snapdragon
Flowering period: mid-June to September.
Colour: red, yellow, pink, white.
Height: 80-100 cm.
Sow under glass in March or outdoors in April. Plant or thin out at 20-25 cm intervals. The plant needs rich soil and a lot of sun. Good cut flower. Pick out first buds for bushier growth and fuller flowering.

ANTIRRHINUM majus nanum maximum
Snapdragon
Flowering period: mid-June to September.
Colour: red, yellow, pink, white.
Height: 40-60 cm.
Sow beginning of March under glass or outside in April. Plant or thin out at 20 cm intervals. Pick out first buds for bushier growth and fuller flowering. The plant needs rich soil and a lot of sun. Good cut flower.

ANTIRRHINUM majus
nanum
Snapdragon
Flowering period: mid-June
to late September.
Colour: red, yellow, pink,
white.
Height: 10-20 cm.
Sow under glass early March or
outside in April. Plant or thin out at
15 cm intervals. The plant bushes
out strongly and spreads well; in a
group of plants it provides a
longlasting carpet of flowers.

AQUILEGIA hybrida
Columbine

Flowering period: May-June.
Colour: red, pink, mauve,
blue, yellow, white.
Height: 45-60 cm.
Sow in the spring. As this is a
perennial, cuttings can be taken.
Columbine needs moist garden
soil in partial shade.

AUBRIETA
Aubrieta

Flowering period: April to
mid-June.
Colour: mauve, violet.
Height: 15 cm.
Sow in seedbed under glass in
March. Plant out in the autumn.
The plant will flower the following
spring. Cuttings from this
perennial can be taken in the
autumn. It is a good spreader and
needs little attention.

BEGONIA semperflorens
Begonia

Flowering period: mid-June
to October.
Colour: white, red, pink.
Height: 25 cm.
Sow January or February in
seedbox. Prick out and late May
plant out at 25 cm intervals. The
plant needs well manured soil,
aerated and moist. A lot of sun.
This begonia is mainly used as a
bedding plant, but also does well
along borders.

BELLIS perennis monstrosa
Daisy

Flowering period: March to
May.
Colour: white, red, pink.
Height: 15 cm.
Sow in a coldtray or outside May-
June. Plant out in the autumn.
First flowering in early spring.
There is also a perennial type, but
those with large blooms will not
survive frosts without great care.

CALENDULA officinalis
Marigold

Flowering period: June to
September.
Colour: orange, yellow,
yellow-white.
Height: up to 30 cm.
Sow in April or May. Plant or thin
out at 25 cm intervals. The
marigold mixes well with many
other summer blooms and is a
beautiful cut flower.

CALLISTEPHUS chinensis
Chinese Aster

Flowering period: July to
October.
Colour: purple, mauve, pink,
white.
Height: up to 30 cm.
Sow under glass in March-April;
outdoors April-May. Plant or thin
out at 20 cm intervals, preferably
in rich soil in a sunny spot.
Delayed sowing gives a somewhat
later flowering time. Good carpet
effect.

CALLISTEPHUS chinensis
Aster

Flowering period: mid-July to
October.
Colour: purple, mauve, pink,
white.
Height: 30-50 cm.
Sow under glass in March-April;
outdoors April-May. Plant or thin
out at 25 cm intervals, preferably
in rich soil in a sunny spot.
Delayed sowing gives a somewhat
later flowering time. Good cut
flower.

CALLISTEPHUS chinensis
Aster

Flowering period: July to
October.
Colour: mauve, red, pink,
yellow.
Height: 50-70 cm.
Sow under glass in March-April;
outdoors April-May. Plant or thin
out at 25 cm intervals, preferably
in rich soil in a sunny spot.
Delayed sowing gives a somewhat
later flowering time. Good cut
flower.

CALLISTEPHUS chinensis
Aster

Flowering period: mid-July to
October.
Colour: mauve, purple, pink,
white.
Height: 50-70 cm.
Sow under glass in March-April;
outdoors April-May. Plant or thin
out at 25 cm intervals, preferably
in rich soil in a sunny spot.
Delayed sowing gives a somewhat
later flowering time. Good cut
flower.

CAMPANULA medium
Canterbury Bell - Single

Flowering period: June to
mid-August.
Colour: white, pink, blue,
mauve.
Height: 60 cm.
Sow in seedbed April-May and
plant out in the autumn. Good cut
flower. They grow in all soils as
long as it is very moist. Shady
spot.

CAMPANULA medium
calycanthema
Canterbury Bell - Double
Flowering period: June to
August.
Colour: white, pink, blue,
mauve.
Height: 70 cm.
Sow in seedbed May-June and
plant out in the autumn at 30 x
30 cm. Grows in most soils as
long as it is very moist. Shady
spot. Good cut flower.

CELOSIA cristata nana
Cockscomb

Flowering period: July to September.
Colour: red, orange, yellow.
Height: 15-25 cm.
Sow under glass in March and later thin out. Plant out in June at 25 cm intervals. An unusual plant adding much decoration to the garden for little attention. But not easy to mix with other plants. Needs a sunny spot.

CELOSIA plumosa pyramidalis
Prince of Wales Feather
Flowering period: July to September.
Colour: red, orange, yellow.
Height: 50-60 cm.
Sow under glass in March, thin out and in June plant out at 30 cm intervals. Suitable as bedding plant and a decorative cut flower. Needs a warm, sheltered spot.

CENTAUREA cyanus
Cornflower

Flowering period: June to October.
Colour: blue, pink, white.
Height: 75 cm.
Sow outside between March and May; thin out to 20-30 cm intervals. For early cut flowers sow in September. Soil should be loose and chalky. Particularly good in a natural garden.

CHEIRANTHUS alllonll
Siberian Wallflower

Flowering period: May to mid-August.
Colour: bright orange-yellow.
Height: 40 cm.
Sow in seedbed and plant out in the autumn. Protect against frost with a layer of twigs. Begins to flower late May and continues all summer. Only cut blooms when they are fully open or stems will be damaged.

CHEIRANTHUS cheiri
Wallflower - Single

Flowering period: April to May.
Colour: crimson, gold, yellow, cream, white.
Height: 20-50 cm.
Sow in May-June and prick out. When seedlings are strong enough, plant out in rich soil in a sunny spot. Protect against frost with a layer of twigs. Only cut blooms when fully open.

CHRYSANTHEMUM carinatum
Marguerite

Flowering period: June to September.
Colour: russet, pink, yellow, white.
Height: 50-60 cm.
Sow in seedbed or outside April-May. Plant or thin out at 25 cm intervals. Loose, well manured soil. In dry periods spray the plant rather than water via the ground. Remove dead blooms. Good cutting flower.

CHRYSANTHEMUM leucan-
themum
Marguerite
Flowering period: June to
August.
Colour: white.
Height: 30-45 cm.
Sow outside in April-May in a
sunny spot with ordinary soil. For
earlier flowering sow under glass
in spring and plant out in May.
This plant is perennial and
cuttings can be taken.

CHRYSANTHEMUM maxi-
mum nanum
Dwarf Marguerite
Flowering period: June to
July.
Colour: white.
Height: 40 cm.
Sow in seedbed in April-May-
June; plant out in the autumn. This
is a perennial needing little
attention. A pre-eminent cut
flower.

CHRYSANTHEMUM multi-
caule
Marguerite
Flowering period: July to
September.
Colour: yellow.
Height: 20-30 cm.
Sow in seedbed or outside April-
May. Plant or thin out at 20 cm
intervals. It needs less attention
than many others of its family.
With moist, loose soil it makes a
good border plant.

CHRYSANTHEMUM segetum
Marguerite

Flowering period: June to
September.
Colour: yellow.
Height: 40-60 cm.
Sow in seedbed or outside April-
May. Plant or thin out at 25 cm
intervals. Loose, well manured
soil. In dry periods spray the plant
rather than water via the ground.
Remove dead blooms. Good cut
flower.

CLARKIA elegans
Clarkia

Flowering period: July to
September.
Colour: crimson, pink, white.
Height: 50-70 cm.
Sow April-May and thin out to 20
cm intervals when seedlings grow
to about 8 cm. Grows best in light,
rich soil with a lot of sun. Mainly
used as bedding plant since they
prefer to stand alone.

CLEOME
Cleome, Spider flower

Flowering period: July to
September.
Colour: pink, white.
Height: 80-100 cm.
Sow under glass in March, plant
out in April-May at 30 cm
intervals. Good border plant with
strong scent.

COSMOS bipinnatus
Cosmos

Flowering period: July to October.
Colour: crimson, pink, white.
Height: 80-120 cm.
Sow under glass from March and plant out in May. In April May sow outdoors. Plant or thin out at 35 cm intervals. Grows in most types of soil. Produces many blooms and is a good cut flower.

DELPHINIUM ajacis
Larkspur

Flowering period: mid-June to September.
Colour: mauve, blue, pink, white.
Height: 120-160 cm.
Sow out April-May. Thin out to 20 cm intervals. Sunny or semi-shady spot. A good cut flower, and some types can be used in rock gardens. This tall plant with its heavy blooms will need some support.

DIANTHUS barbatus
Sweet William

Flowering period: June to October.
Colour: crimson, scarlet, red, pink, white.
Height: 20-40 cm.
Sow in a sunny spot in March or April, thin out and replant at 20 cm intervals in June. Prefers well-drained soil. Good cut flower.

DIANTHUS barbatus
Sweet William - single

Flowering period: late May to mid-July.
Colour: mixed pink, red, white, lilac, purple.
Height: 50 cm.
Sow outdoors and transplant to intervals of 10 x 10 cm. In the autumn replant to 25 x 25 cm. This biennial flowers from May, preferably in clay'ey soil and in a sunny, sheltered spot. Good cut flower.

DIANTHUS barbatus
Sweet William - double

Flowering period: May to mid-September.
Colour: crimson, scarlet, pink, white.
Height: 10-60 cm.
Sow in outside seedbed, prick out and in October replant at 20 cm intervals in a sunny, sheltered spot. Dianthus thrives in heavy soil. Good cut flower.

DIANTHUS caryophyllus
Carnation

Flowering period: August to September.
Colour: pink, crimson, yellow, white.
Height: 30-60 cm.
Sow under glass in February-March. Plant out in May to a sunny, sheltered spot. Dianthus thrives in heavy soil. Carnations are mostly grown in greenhouses for cutting, but also do well in gardens.

DIANTHUS chinensis
heddewigii
Chinese Carnation
Flowering period: July to
September.
Colour: crimson, pink, white.
Height: 20-35 cm.
Sow under glass in March-April;
plant out in May at 15 cm
intervals, in a sunny spot. Well-
drained soil.

DIGITALIS purpurea
Foxglove
Flowering period: June-July.
Colour: pink, yellow, cream,
white.
Height: 150-180 cm.
Sow outdoors in May or June for
flowering the following years.
Ordinary garden soil, in the sun or
partial shade. As well as this
biennial type there is also one
from which cuttings can be taken.

DIMORPHOTHECA
Dimorphotheca
Flowering period: July to
September.
Colour: orange, pink, yellow.
Height: 25-30 cm.
Sow in seedbed or outside in
April-May and plant out late May
at 15 cm intervals. Does not like
rain and sun is essential for fully
opened flowers. Flourishes in
light, well-drained soil.

DORONICUM caucasicum
Leopard's Bane

Flowering period: April-May.
Colour: deep yellow.
Height: 30-40 cm.
Sow outdoors in May-June;
replant in September for a first
flowering the following spring.
Cuttings can be taken in the
autumn. The plant flourishes in
shade and is therefore excellent for
town gardens.

ESCHSCHOLZIA californica
Californian Poppy

Flowering period: June to
September.
Colour: orange, yellow,
crimson.
Height: 20-45 cm.
Sow in March-April in ordinary
garden soil in a sunny spot. Thin
out to 15 cm intervals. An easy to
grow plant yielding many blooms,
that does well amongst other
flowers of similar height.

GAILLARDIA pulchella picta
Gaillardia

Flowering period: July to
September.
Colour: purple, white.
Height: 60-85 cm.
Sow under glass in March and
plant out in May to well-drained
soil. Support for the plant is
recommended. Good cut flower.

GAZANIA splendens
Gazania

Flowering period: July to September.
Colour: orange
Height: 15-25 cm.
Sow under glass in February or March or outside in April. Plant out seedlings in May, in chalky ground in a sunny spot. Take cuttings in August. Raise in frost-free atmosphere, in two parts loam, one part peat and one part sand.

GODETIA hybrida
Godetia

Flowering period: July to September.
Colour: dark red, orange, white.
Height: 25-60 cm.
Sow under glass early April, or in a sunny outside spot April-May. Thin out to 20 cm intervals. The tall azaleas are for cutting, whilst the shorter types are good in flowerbeds.

GYPSOPHILA elegans
Baby's Breath

Flowering period: May to September.
Colour: white to pale pink.
Height: 30-45 cm.
Between April and mid-July sow outside, and later thin out. Suitable for rock gardens with chalky soil, particularly the dwarf type. But the taller types are also good cut flowers.

GYPSOPHILA paniculata
Maiden's Breath

Flowering period: July to August.
Colour: white.
Height: 90 cm.
Sow in seedbed in May-July, thin out slightly and transplant to chosen spot with 35 x 35 cm gaps in the autumn. Take cuttings from the roots late summer. Flowers are good for both cutting and drying.

HELIANTHEMUM mutabile
Rock Rose

Flowering period: June to July.
Colour: white, pink, scarlet, yellow.
Height: 15-25 cm.
Sow in seedbed May-June, thin out slightly and transplant in the autumn at 20 x 20 cm. The rock rose is a perennial and cuttings can be taken in the autumn. For a really full bloom a sunny, sheltered spot is essential.

HELIANTHUS annuus
Common Sunflower

Flowering period: July to October.
Colour: yellow, chestnut to white with brown centre.
Height: 300-350 cm.
Sow in April in clay'ey soil. Water well using liquid manure to promote the growth. The seed of the sunflower makes good bird food.

HELIANTHUS cucumerifolius
Miniature Sunflower

Flowering period: June to
August.
Colour: yellow with brown
centre.
Height: 90-120 cm.
Sow in April in clay'ey soil in the
full sun. This type is good for cut
flower.

HELIANTHUS giganteus
Giant Sunflower

Flowering period: July to
October.
Colour: yellow.
Height: 200-300 cm.
Sow outside in April, preferably in
clay'ey soil and in the full sun.
Because of its height, it does best
in a sheltered spot, supported by a
stick. Needs feeding, and now and
then some manure.

HELICHRYSUM bract.mon-
strosum
Everlasting Flower
Flowering period: July to
October.
Colour: yellow, white, pink,
scarlet, silver.
Height: 30 cm.
Sow under glass between mid-
March and mid-April and plant out
early May. Or sow outdoors
between mid-April and mid-May.
Thin out to 15 cm intervals.
Drying: hang tied bunches upside
down.

IBERIS umbellata
Candytuft

Flowering period: July to
August.
Colour: bright red, pink,
white.
Height: 25 cm.
Sow in March or April in light soil.
Thin out seedlings to 5 cm
intervals. Keep soil moist. Candytuft can be replanted into beds,
along borders or used in rock
gardens; in warm, sunny spots.

IMPATIENS walleriana
Busy Lizzie

Flowering period: July to
October.
Colour: scarlet, pink, white.
Height: 30-90 cm.
Sow in the garden April or early
May, in a sunny spot. Thin out to
15 cm intervals. Can be raised as
border plant and can take light
shade.

IPOMOEA purpurea
Morning Glory

Flowering period: July to
September.
Colour: purple, lilac, pink,
white.
Height: climber, to 300 cm.
Sow under glass in March, or
outside in May in a sheltered,
sunny spot in rich, moist soil.
Does best up a south wall or fence
with wire netting support.

LATHYRUS odoratus
gigantea
Giant Sweet Pea
Flowering period: June to
September.
Colour: blue
Height: 150 cm.
Sow outside early spring in chalky
ground. Feed with solution of
liquid manure. The giant sweet pea
needs support; usually wire-
netting. A good cut flower.

LATHYRUS spencer
Sweet Pea
Flowering period: June to
August.
Colour: crimson
Height: 30 cm.
Sow under glass early spring and
plant out seedlings in May; or sow
outside in the cold ground in April.
All soil types are suitable. Plants
need some support. Good cut
flower.

LAVATERA trimestris
Tree Mallow
Flowering period: July to
October.
Colour: pink
Height: 120-140 cm.
Sow under glass in March and
plant out in May. Or sow outdoors
mid-April to late May. Thin out to
40 x 40 cm intervals. The plants
like a warm, dry spot.

LEONTOPODIUM alpinum
Edelweiss

Flowering period: June to
August.
Colour: silver.
Height: 10-30 cm.
Sow under glass in March (or
outside in April). Plant out in the
autumn. Edelweiss needs chalky
ground and is most suitable for
rock gardens.

LIATRIS spicata
Liatris, Blazing Star

Flowering period: July to
September.
Colour: bright mauve.
Height: 60-90 cm.
Sow outside in March or April.
Flowering occurs the following
year. The plant is a perennial, and
although the soil should be dry the
root will survive the winter. Needs
a sunny spot and light soil.

LINARIA maroccana
Toadflax

Flowering period: July to
September.
Colour: mixed: crimson,
orange, mauve, white.
Height: 30 cm.
Sow directly outdoors April-May.
Very suitable for sunny border or
rock garden. Because of its short
flowering time, sowing at intervals
of a month will lengthen the
blooming period.

LINUM perenne
Flax

Flowering period: June to August.
Colour: bright blue.
Height: 70 cm.
Sow in seedbed in April-May-June. Transplant in the autumn. A perennial, flax needs a lot of sun and light, well-drained soil. The colour shows up particularly well amongst herbs.

LOBELIA erinus compacta
Lobelia

Flowering period: June to mid-September.
Colour: blue.
Height: 15 cm.
Sow in February in a seedbox under glass and plant out in May. Thin out (as bedding plant) to 20 cm intervals. Lobelia spreads well and is therefore suitable for rock gardens.

LOBELIA pendula
Hanging Lobelia

Flowering period: June to mid-September.
Colour: blue.
Height: 15-30 cm.
Sow in February in a seedbox under glass. This hanging lobelia is extremely good in hung containers or along a small wall.

LONAS inodora
Lonas

Flowering period: July to September.
Colour: yellow.
Height: 20-30 cm.
Sow early March under glass. Plant out between May and June in groups at 10 x 10 cm. For a longer blooming period, cut off dead flowers. Much cultivated as a cut flower, it also makes a good dry flower.

LUNARIA biennis
Honesty

Flowering period: June to July.
Colour: violet.
Height: 100 cm.
Sow April to mid-June and plant out in a shady spot in the autumn. Honesty is very decorative particularly in bouquets of dry flowers. The plant must be tied up after flowering to protect the delicate fruit.

LUPINUS hartwegii
Lupin

Flowering period: July to October.
Colour: blue, yellow, red.
Height: 60-90 cm.
Sow in April in rows in a seedbed. In May prick out to 20-25 cm intervals. It is important to remove dead pods to ensure a full bloom. Lupins improve the soil and are good cut flowers.

LUPINUS polyphyllus
Lupin

Flowering period: June to mid-August.
Colour: blue, mauve, pink, yellow, white.
Height: 50 cm.
Sow in seedbed April-May-June and plant out in the autumn to light, sandy soil in a sunny spot. Cuttings should be taken in April.

MATRICARIA eximia nana
Matricaria

Flowering period: July to September.
Colour: lemon yellow.
Height: 30 cm.
Sow in March or April in a seedbed and plant out. First blooms show in May. A good flower for filling in between other plants for seed.

MATTHIOLA incana
Stock

Flowering period: July to September.
Colour: purple, white, pink, red.
Height: 45 cm.
Sow under glass in March-April; plant out in May to well fertilized soil. For good growth add a quick working nitrogen fertilizer. Keep the soil moist. Stock is mainly grown as a cut flower.

MESEMBRYANTHEMUM
Mesembryanthemum

Flowering period: mid-June to late August.
Colour: pink, white, rose, red.
Height: 15 cm.
Sow under glass in March-April and plant out in May. Or sow outside in April-May. Thin out to 30 x 30 cm. Choose a sunny spot. Suitable for flowerbed or rock garden.

MIRABILIS jalapa
Mirabilis

Flowering period: July to early October.
Colour: mauve, red, yellow, white.
Height: 60-90 cm.
Sow under glass in March-April and plant out mid-May. Or sow outside in a seedbed or in rows. Plant or thin out to 35 x 35 cm. Needs rich soil and a sunny spot.

MYOSOTIS alpestris
Forget-me-not

Flowering period: April to June.
Colour: blue, pale pink, white.
Height: 15-25 cm.
Sow in May or June and plant out in moist soil in the autumn. First flowering of this biennial follows in the spring. It needs a shady spot and chalky, moist soil. The colours make it a lovely background for tulips.

NEMESIA strumosa compacta
Nemesia
Flowering period: June to September.
Colour: orange, crimson, mauve, yellow, white.
Height: 20 cm.
Sow in March-April in seedbed under glass or outdoors. Plant out to a sunny spot in the border, or thin out if sown outside. Does not like a lot of moisture.

NEPETA mussini

Flowering period: June to August.
Colour: blue.
Height: 30 cm.
Sow in seedbed April-May-June and plant out in the autumn. A perennial, cuttings can be taken in the spring. Needs a lot of sun and dry soil. Suitable for heather garden or borders.

NICOTIANA alata
Ornamental Tobacco
Flowering period: July to September.
Colour: green-white, pink, red.
Height: 60-90 cm.
Sow in February-March in a warm greenhouse. Plant out late May in the sun or partial shade. The plant needs fertile soil and sufficient moisture.

NIGELLA damascena
Love-in-a-Mist

Flowering period: July to September.
Colour: pink, white, blue.
Height: 45 cm.
Sow outdoors between mid-April and mid-May; thin out to 25 x 15 cm. This is a good cutting flower and can also be used for drying. It needs sun and a chalky, moist soil.

PAPAVER rhoeas
Field Poppy

Flowering period: July to October.
Colour: scarlet.
Height: 15 cm.
Sow under glass in February-March and plant out in May. All soils can be used but poppies like a lot of sun. When used as a cut flower it is advisable to cauterize the stem before putting it in water.

PAPAVER somniferum
Opium Poppy

Flowering period: July to October.
Colour: pale lilac, purple, white.
Height: 60-90 cm.
Sow in chosen spot in April. Thin out when the seedlings reach a height of 5 to 8 cm. They require a sunny place and fairly good soil.

PELARGONIUM
Geranium

Flowering period: July to October.
Colour: pink, red, white.
Height: 35 cm.
Sow between January and April in a heated seedtray. Prick out seedlings and transfer to fairly large pots. There are more than 300 different members of the Pelargonium family. It is a strong plant with many uses.

PETUNIA nana compacta
Petunia

Flowering period: June to October.
Colour: mauve, white, red, pink, violet or a two-colour mix.
Height: 25 cm.
Sow in seedtray in March-April, plant out in a mixture of clay, leaf mould and sand. In summer feed with liquid manure about twice a week.

PETUNIA pendula
Hanging Petunia

Flowering period: June to October.
Colour: violet, pink, red, white or two-colour mix.
Height: hanging plant.
Sow under glass or outside between January and March, and thin out in April-May. This hanging petunia is particularly suitable for troughs along walls or fences.

PHLOX drummondii
Phlox

Flowering period: July to August.
Colour: combination of red, pink, violet, white.
Height: 30 cm.
Sow under glass in March. Plant out in June in a sunny spot at 15 cm intervals. Pick out the top of the plant for a bushier growth. It grows best in chalky soil. A good border plant.

PHLOX drummondii cuspidate
Phlox

Flowering period: July to August.
Colour: mixed; red-pink-white-violet.
Height: 15 cm.
Sow in March under glass. Plant out in June in a sunny spot at 15 cm intervals. It grows best in chalky soil, and is a good border plant.

PHYSALIS franchettii
Chinese Lantern

Flowering period: June.
Colour: white (flower), orange (fruit).
Height: 45-100 cm.
Sow early spring in sandy soil in a sunny or semi-shady spot. An easy plant to grow but inclined to spread. Take care it does not take over. The fruit, the lanterns, are easy to dry.

PORTULACA grandiflora
Portulaca, Sun Plant

Flowering period: mid-July to mid-October.
Colour: yellow, white, pink, red, orange.
Height: 15 cm.
Sow under glass or outdoors in March-April. Very suitable for rock gardens. They prefer a sunny spot in sandy soil.

PRIMULA acaulis
Primrose

Flowering period: mid-March to late May.
Colour: crimson, pink, yellow, blue, white.
Height: 20-30 cm.
Sow under glass between February and April, prick out and plant out in the autumn. Needs moist, heavy soil. Perennial, so cuttings can be taken; store in a cold-frame for the winter.

PRIMULA denticulata
Primula

Flowering period: March to May.
Colour: lilac.
Height: 30 cm.
Sow under glass in February-March. Transplant outside in June and plant out in October. Needs light but not full sun. Preferably heavy, fairly moist soil. Perennial, but store in cold-frame during winters.

PRIMULA veris
Cowslip

Flowering period: March to May.
Colour: red, orange, yellow, blue, violet.
Height: 30 cm.
Sow in seedtray, prick out and plant out in the autumn. Like the primrose an early bloomer. Store in coldframe in winter, since this plant can suffer from too much moisture.

RESEDA odorata
Mignonette

Flowering period: June to October.
Colour: white-yellow.
Height: 35 cm.
Sow under glass in April-May or outside late April. Thin out to 20 x 15 cm. Mignonette needs rich, not too damp soil. Grows in sun or partial shade. The flowers have a pleasant perfume.

RHODANTHE manglesii
Rhodanthe

Flowering period: June to September.
Colour: pink.
Height: 40 cm.
Sow in March-April under glass and plant out early May. Or sow in rows outside in April-May. Thin out to 25 x 15 cm. A nice, but delicate, dry flower.

RUDBECKIA hirta
Black-Eyed Susan

Flowering period: July to mid-October.
Colour: gold-orange, mahogany.
Height: 80 cm.
Sow in seedbed in March-April, under glass or outside, preferably in a sunny spot. The plant flourishes in chalky soil.

SALPIGLOSSIS sinuata
Salpiglossis

Flowering period: mid-June to October.
Colour: rose-red, crimson, purple-yellow, cream.
Height: 50 cm.
Sow under glass in seedbed in March, or outside during April, in a mixture of leaf mould, peat and sharp sand in equal parts.

SALVIA splendens compacta
Salvia

Flowering period: June to October.
Colour: scarlet.
Height: 30 cm.
Sow under glass in February-April. Plant out at intervals of 20 x 20 cm. Salvia is easy to grow and thrives in well-drained garden soil.

SAPONARIA
Soapwort

Flowering period: June to mid-August.
Colour: pink.
Height: 30 cm.
Sow in seedbed between April and June and plant out in the autumn. A perennial, most suitable for rock gardens or for wall troughs.

SAXIFRAGA
Floral Carpet

Flowering period: May to June.
Colour: pink, white, red.
Height: 20 cm.
Sow under glass in April-May. Prick out and transplant to seedbed. Plant out in the autumn at 15 x 15 cm intervals, in well-drained ground in partial shade. A perennial and a good spreader.

SCABIOSA atropurpurea
Scabious

Flowering period: July to September.
Colour: dark purple-red.
Height: 60-90 cm.
Sow under glass in February. Plant out in May to good, chalky soil. The plants yield a mass of blooms which cutting merely increases. But take care with the stems which are delicate.

STATICE sinuatum
Statice

Flowering period: August to October.
Colour: pink, lavender blue, white.
Height: 15-20 cm.
Sow under glass in April and plant out mid-May to a sunny spot with well-drained soil. Statice is amongst the prettiest of flowers and one of the most suitable for drying.

TAGETES erecta
African Marigolds

Flowering period: July to September.
Colour: yellow, orange.
Height: varies from 30-100 cm.
Sow under glass in February-March and plant out late May or June. Or sow outside from May in a sunny spot. The plant does not like rain, and prefers heat and dryness.

TAGETES erecta nana
Dwarf Marigold

Flowering period: mid-June to October.
Colour: yellow.
Height: 20 cm.
Sow March-April under glass and plant out in May. Thin out at intervals of 25 x 25 cm. The sap from the roots retards the growth of weeds and kills harmful ground heels; a useful plant.

TAGETES signata pumila
Single Marigold

Flowering period: mid-June to mid-October.
Colour: golden yellow.
Height: 25 cm.
Sow in seedbed March-April-May and plant out; or in chosen spot from April and thin out in May. Sensitive to rain, but likes heat and dryness. Otherwise needs little attention.

THYMUS
Thyme

Flowering period: mid-June to August.
Colour: purple, pink.
Height: 10 cm.
Sow in seedbed between April and June. Plant out in the autumn. Suitable for rock gardens. Grows over stones and rocks. Needs good drainage and a sunny spot. This hardy perennial will withstand winters.

TRITOMA
Tritoma

Flowering period: June to mid-October.
Colour: orange-red-yellow tints.
Height: 80 cm.
Sow in seedbed between April and June. Plant out in the autumn. Sheltered, sunny spot with good drainage. Cover in winter. Cuttings can be taken spring and autumn. Perennial.

TROPAEOLUM majus
Nasturtium

Flowering period: mid-June
to October.
Colour: scarlet, mahogany,
red, yellow, cream, white.
Height: 150 cm (climber).
Sow in garden in April or May.
Grows well in poor soil but needs
a lot of sun. Will change a bare
wall into a curtain of flowers.

TROPAEOLUM majus nanum
Nasturtium

Flowering period: July to
October.
Colour: scarlet, mahogany,
red, yellow, cream, white.
Height: 30 cm.
Sow outside in April-May,
preferably in rows. Thin out to
about 20 cm. The plant does well
in poor soil.

VERBENA hybrida compacta
Verbena

Flowering period: July to
October.
Colour: scarlet, crimson,
blue, white.
Height: 30 cm.
Sow under glass in February-
March and plant out to well-
drained soil in May or June. The
flowers have fresh, bright colours.

VERONICA spicata
Spiked Speedwell

Flowering period: July to
September.
Colour: white, blue, pink, red.
Height: 30-60 cm.
Sow in seedbed between May and
July, slightly thin out and plant out
in the autumn to 20 x 20 cm in
well-drained soil in a sunny spot.
Perennial.

VIOLA cornuta
Pansy

Flowering period: April to
October.
Colour: three shades of
mauve.
Height: 15 cm.
Sow under glass in seedbed in
February-March, or late summer
in moist, rich soil. Old clumps can
be taken out. After flowering cut
the plant to ground level. Perennial. Cover lightly in winter.

VIOLA tricolor maxima
Wild Pansy

Flowering period: June to
October.
Colour: three shades; yellow-
blue, mauve, brown, cream;
dark purple centre.
Height: 25 cm.
Annual: sow under glass
February-March and plant out
April-May. Biennial: June-July in
seedbed. Plant out before or after
the winter. In winter cover against
frost.

VIOLA tricolor maxima
Giant Pansy

Flowering period: June to
October.
Colour: brown-blue, yellow,
white.
Height: 15 cm.
Sow under glass in February-
March and plant out April-May
(annual). Or outside in July and
plant out before or after the winter
(bi- or perennial). Cover in winter
against frost.

XERANTHEMUM annuum
Xeranthemum

Flowering period: July to
August.
Colour: pink, white, yellow.
Height: up to 50 cm.
Sow in April in a sunny spot in
slightly moist soil. This is a flower
for drying. Cut blooms as they
open and dry hanging upside
down in an airy place out of the
sun.

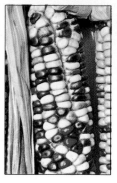

ZEA japonica
Ornamental Maize

Flowering period: July to
September.
Colour: seeds in the cobs vary
from dark brown and red to
orange, light and deep yellow.
Height: 150 cm.
Sow late April-early May outside
in rows. Thin out to 30 cm. Well
dug ground with plenty of organic
manure.

ZINNIA elegans
Giant Zinnia

Flowering period: July to
October.
Colour: pink, red, cream,
orange, light brown, lilac.
Height: 75 cm.
Sow March-April under glass, or
late April-early May in rows
outdoors. Thin out to 35 x 20 cm.
Good drainage and liquid fertilizer
benefit the plant. Because of their
size and weight, the flowers may
need support.

ZINNIA elegans
Zinnia

Flowering period: July to
October.
Colour: red, yellow, lilac.
Height: 30-100 cm (diameter
can be 12 cm).
Sow under glass in March-April.
Not easy to transplant, it is best to
pot them and transfer plant with all
its soil to the garden. Seeds can be
sown out in May. Feed with
solution of liquid manure.

ZINNIA elegans 'Thumbelina'
Dwarf Zinnia

Flowering period: June to
October.
Colour: scarlet, pink, yellow,
white.
Height: 15 cm.
Sow under glass in March or
outside in May. Plant or thin out
late May. During the summer
months water periodically with
solution of liquid manure.

Everyone knows the tulip, hyacinth, daffodil and crocus; but did you know that there are at least 100 other bulbs and tubers; from small to large, from early to late blooming, with a large variety of flower shape and colour? We cannot show them all in this guide, but on the following pages you will probably find several varieties that you did not know before.

The best known of the bulbs are those that appear early in spring bringing a touch of colour to the snow covered or grey earth. Later, the tulips and daffodils appear, and from then on bulbs and tubers take their place between the other plants in your garden. Most of them need little attention, apart from fertile, loose soil. The young shoot has to push its way up through the earth – and still retain enough strength for the plant to grow and flower. Planting takes place in autumn, around October-November, preferably in groups. It is important to plant the bulb at the correct depth; you will find this information in the text. Let the shoot die off to conserve the strength of the bulb.

ACIDANTHERA bicolor murielae
Abyssinian Gladiolus
Flowering period: September to October.
Colour: white.
Height: 40-60 cm.
Plant gladioli bulbs late April, 5 cm deep at 5 cm intervals, in a sunny place. They prefer a sheltered spot in well-drained soil. Lift and dry in winter and store in a tray with some peat mould.

ALLIUM giganteum
Allium
Flowering period: June to July.
Colour: lilac.
Height: 175 cm.
Plant in autumn 5 to 15 cm deep at 5 to 30 cm intervals in well-drained soil in a fairly sunny spot. Good cut flower. Cover bulbs warmly in winter with straw, hay or peat mould.

ALLIUM moly
Allium
Flowering period: May to June.
Colour: golden yellow.
Height: 25 cm.
Plant in autumn 5 cm deep at 5 cm intervals in well-drained soil in a rather sheltered spot in partial shade in rock garden. Cover against frost in winter with straw or peat mould.

ANEMONE blanda
Windflower

Flowering period: February to April.
Colour: pale to deep blue, mauve, pink, white.
Height: 10-15 cm.
Plant in spring, 2 to 5 cm deep. Plant new bulbs each spring in cold soil with humus in full sun. Cover with leaf mould in very cold weather. Good cut flower.

ANEMONE coronaria-hybride
Windflower (double)

Flowering period: February to May.
Colour: white, mauve, scarlet.
Height: 15-30 cm.
Plant in spring, 2 to 5 cm deep. Plant new bulbs each spring in cold soil with humus in full sun. Cover with leaf mould in very cold weather. Good cut flower.

ANEMONE coronaria-hybride
Windflower (single)

Flowering period: February to May.
Colour: white, mauve, scarlet.
Height: 15-30 cm.
Plant in spring, 2 to 5 cm deep. Plant new bulbs each spring in cold soil with humus in full sun. Cover with leaf mould in very cold weather. Good cut flower.

BEGONIA grandiflora
Begonia - double

Flowering period: June to July.
Colour: yellow, white, red.
Height: 25 cm.
Plant indoors in large pots in a mixture of peat and sand in March-April. Once night frosts are over, plant out in moist soil and protect from wind and too much sun. Lift the bulbs in October and store in peat mould.

BRODIAEA
Brodiaea

Flowering period: June.
Colour: violet-blue.
Height: about 60 cm.
Plant in September 7 cm deep in well-drained soil not too far apart (about 3 cm); preferably under shrubs in a sheltered spot. Lift and dry the bulbs in winter and store indoors.

CANNA
Canna

Flowering period: June to September.
Colour: red.
Height: about 120 cm.
Plant in a pot March-April in moist soil in a temperature of 16 to 21° with sufficient light. Plant out late May in bed or border in a sheltered spot in sun or partial shade. Root stocks need a moist covering in winter.

CHIONODOXA luciliae
Glory of the Snow

Flowering period: March.
Colour: sky blue.
Height: 15 cm,
Plant out in autumn in fertile soil in sun or partial shade. If the seed is allowed to ripen, the plant will propagate itself. Plant the bulbs 2 to 5 cm deep at 5 cm intervals.

CONVALLARIA majalis
Lily of the Valley

Flowering period: April to May.
Colour: white.
Height: 15-25 cm.
Plant spring or autumn in humus rich, fertilised soil, 2 cm deep and at 10 to 15 cm intervals; under shrubs or in a shady spot. After 3 or 4 years the plant will run wild and create a lovely carpet of tiny lilies.

CROCUS specie
Crocus

Flowering period: February to March.
Colour: yellow, white, purple
Height: about 7 cm.
Crocuses prefer to grow in the sun. Plant bulbs in October 5 to 8 cm deep in small groups in well-drained soil. They can be planted amongst other spreading plants or in the lawn.

CROCUS striped banner
Crocus - striped

Flowering period: February to March.
Colour: striped white, purple.
Height: about 7 cm.
Crocuses prefer to grow in the sun. Plant bulbs in October 5 to 8 cm deep in small groups in well-drained soil. They can be planted amongst other spreading plant or in the lawn.

CYCLAMEN
Cyclamen

Flowering period: February to March.
Colour: pink.
Height: 5-12 cm.
Plant cyclamen in August-September in loamy, humus rich, well-drained soil. Cover well with leaf mould in winter. A nice rock garden plant.

DAHLIA
Dahlia - top mix

Flowering period: July to September.
Colour: yellow, pink, red, white.
Height: about 45 cm.
Plant out May or June in well fertilised soil in sun, at 55 cm intervals. Three weeks later pinch out tops to promote growth of sideshoots. Needs some support. Lift tubers before winter. Good cut flower.

DAHLIA
Dahlia - pompom

Flowering period: July to September.
Colour: red with white.
Height: up to 90 cm.
Plant out May or June in well fertilised soil in sun, at 90 cm intervals. Three weeks later pinch out tops to promote growth of sideshoots. Needs some support. Lift tubers before winter. Good cut flower.

DAHLIA
Dahlia - decorative

Flowering period: July to September.
Colour: red with white petal tips.
Height: 90-150 cm.
Plant out May or June in well fertilised soil in sun, at 90 cm intervals. Three weeks later pinch out tops to promote growth of sideshoots. Needs some support. Lift tubers before winter.

DAHLIA
Dahlia - cactus

Flowering period: July to September.
Colour: mixed red-yellow-pink-orange-white.
Height: 90-150 cm.
Plant out May or June in well fertilised soil in sun, at 90 cm intervals. Three weeks later pinch out tops to promote growth of sideshoots. Needs some support. Lift tubers before winter.

ERANTHIS hyemalis
Winter Aconite

Flowering period: February to March.
Colour: bright golden yellow.
Height: 5-8 cm.
Plant tubers September-October, 5 to 7 cm deep in loamy soil in a fairly moist spot, under shrubs or trees. Propagate by dividing tubers; but the plant will also reproduce itself.

EREMURUS
Foxtail Lily

Flowering period: June.
Colour: yellow, white, pink, orange.
Height: 100-150 cm.
A large hole must be dug, 75 cm deep. Cover bottom with sand; add a mixture of peat mould and manure. Also put a layer of sand around the tubers. Cover against frosts. The plant loves sun and is a good cut flower. Propagate by splitting.

FREESIA
Freesia

Flowering period: July to October.
Colour: white-yellow-orange.
Height: about 40 cm.
Sow freesias in greenhouse in March. Plant out in summer in slightly moist soil in sun or partial shade, at 20 cm intervals. Some support is necessary. After flowering, fertilise the tubers. Good cut flower.

LILIUM aziaticum hybride
Eastern Lily

Flowering period: June.
Colour: orange-red.
Height: 90-150 cm.
Needs soil well dug with leaf
mould, peat and soft manure.
Plant deep (20 cm) at 12 to 35 cm
intervals, between October and
March in partial shade. Propagate
by planting small side bulbs in a
coldtray.

LILIUM henryi
Lily

Flowering period: July to
September.
Colour: orange.
Height: up to 150 cm.
Thrives in well-drained soil with
lime. Plant bulbs 20 cm deep at
30 cm intervals in partial shade.
Cover with leaf mould in winter.
Propagate from side bulbs or
seed, using sandy soil.

LILIUM martagon album
Turkish Lily

Flowering period: July.
Colour: white.
Height: 150 cm.
Plant in lime rich soil 20 cm deep
at 30 cm intervals in partial shade.
Cover with leaves between October
and March. Propagate by taking
side bulbs during flowering and
planting in coldframe.

MUSCARI armeniacum
Grape Hyacinth

Flowering period: April to
May.
Colour: pale and dark blue.
Height: 20-25 cm.
Plant small bulbs September-
October 5 to 7 cm deep at 7 cm
intervals in ordinary soil in the
sun. Suitable for rock garden;
easily runs wild. Propagate by
dividing the clumps in July.

MUSCARI album
Grape Hyacinth

Flowering period: April to
May.
Colour: white.
Height: 20-25 cm.
Plant small bulbs September-
October 5 to 7 cm deep at 7 cm
intervals in ordinary soil In the
sun. Suitable for rock garden;
easily runs wild. Propagate by
dividing the clumps in July.

NARCISSUS actaea
Daffodil

Flowering period: April.
Colour: white, with orange-
red.
Height: about 25 cm.
Plant bulbs early, September-
October, in fertile, well-drained
soil, 10 cm deep at 20 cm
intervals, in the sun. After
flowering let leaves die off. This
daffodil looks after itself; but give
it some fertiliser each year.

NARCISSUS cyclamineus
Daffodil

Flowering period: February to March.
Colour: yellow.
Height: 20-40 cm.
Plant bulbs early, September-October, in fertile, well-drained soil, 10 cm deep at 20 cm intervals, in the sun. After flowering let leaves die off. This daffodil looks after itself; but give it some fertiliser each year.

NARCISSUS fortune
Daffodil

Flowering period: March to May.
Colour: yellow with orange trumpet.
Height: 35-50 cm.
Plant bulbs early, September-October, in fertile, well-drained soil, 10 cm deep at 20 cm intervals, in the sun. Plant in small groups. After flowering let leaves die off. Propagate from side bulbs. Fertilise each year.

NARCISSUS golden harvest
Daffodil

Flowering period: March to May.
Colour: yellow.
Height: 35-50 cm.
Plant bulbs early, September-October, in fertile, well-drained soil, 10 cm deep at 20 cm intervals, in the sun. Plant in small groups. After flowering let leaves die off. Propagate from side bulbs. Do not leave to run wild.

NARCISSUS yellow cheerfulness
Daffodil
Flowering period: April.
Colour: pale yellow.
Height: 20-40 cm.
Plant bulbs early, September-October, in fertile, well-drained soil, 10 cm deep at 20 cm intervals, in the sun. After flowering let leaves die off. This daffodil looks after itself. Propagate from side bulbs.

ORNITHOGALUM
Star of Bethlehem

Flowering period: April to May.
Colour: white.
Height: 35-45 cm.
Plant in October in light, humus rich soil in partial shade, 7 to 14 cm deep at 5 to 7 cm intervals. Suitable for rock garden and good cut flower. Lift bulbs in November and store in frost free place.

OXALIS deppei
Four Leafed Clover

Flowering period: May to July.
Colour: pink.
Height: 12-20 cm.
Plant clover in October in sun or partial shade, 5 to 7 cm deep at 5 to 10 cm intervals in well-drained soil. Suitable for rock garden and winter hard.

PUSCHKINIA libanotica
Striped Squill

Flowering period: April.
Colour: bluish-white.
Height: 15 cm.
Plant in October, 5 cm deep at 7 cm intervals in sun or partial shade in ordinary garden soil. Propagate from side bulbs; or from seed sown in July in a coldframe; only plant out after two years growth, again in July.

RANUNCULUS
Buttercup

Flowering period: June to July.
Colour: white, red, orange, pink.
Height: about 40 cm.
Plant in April 2 cm deep at 7 cm intervals in clay'ey soil that must be moist. It likes either sun or partial shade. The tubers are not easy to keep; it is better to plant new each year. Good cut flower.

SCILLA campanulata
Squill

Flowering period: March to April.
Colour: white, blue, pink.
Height: 50 cm.
Plant in October 5 to 7 cm deep at 7 to 25 cm intervals in loose, humus rich soil that retains its moisture in partial shade. Propagate from side bulbs.

SCILLA sibirica
Squill

Flowering period: March to April.
Colour: blue.
Height: 15-20 cm.
Plant in October 5 to 7 cm deep at 15 to 25 cm intervals in loose, humus rich soil that retains its moisture in partial shade. Propagate from side bulbs.

SPARAXIS tricolor
Harlequin Flower

Flowering period: May to June.
Colour: red, white, purple, yellow.
Height: 30-45 cm.
Plant the tubers in November in well-drained soil, 7 to 10 cm deep at 7 cm intervals in full sun. When leaf dies off in July, lift and dry tubers for storage until November. Good cut flower.

TULIPA arabian mystery
Tulip

Flowering period: late April.
Colour: red, with white petal edges.
Height: 30-45 cm.
A hybrid of several early tulips and the Darwin tulip, distinguished by the colour change on its petal edges. Plant in October 7 cm deep at 10 cm intervals in light, lime rich soil in sun or partial shade. Winter hard and good cut flower.

TULIPA Bernhard van Leer
Tulip - Darwin

Flowering period: late April to early May.
Colour: red.
Height: 60-70 cm.
Darwin is the 'ordinary' tulip with bold colours. Plant October 8 cm deep at 10 cm intervals, preferably in groups. Tulips grow best in light, lime rich soil in sun or partial shade. Good cut flower.

TULIPA china pink
Tulip

Flowering period: May.
Colour: pink.
Height: 40-60 cm.
A lily-like tulip, with pointed, outward curving petals. Plant in October 7 cm deep at 10 cm intervals, in light, lime rich soil, preferably in groups, in sun or partial shade. Good cut flower.

TULIPA eros
Tulip - double, late

Flowering period: May.
Colour: pink.
Height: 45-60 cm.
Double, late blooming tulips with flowers rather like peonies. Plant bulbs in October 8 cm deep at 10 cm intervals, preferably in groups. They do best in light, lime rich soil in sun or partial shade. Winter hard and good cut flower.

TULIPA fringed beauty
Tulip - double, early

Flowering period: April.
Colour: red with yellow.
Height: 20-30 cm.
Double, early blooming tulips with flowers rather like peonies. Plant bulbs in October 8 cm deep at 10 cm intervals, preferably in groups. They do best in light, lime rich soil in sun or partial shade. Winter hard and good cut flower.

TULIPA tarda
Tulip

Flowering period: early April.
Colour: cream-yellow.
Height: 15 cm.
Plant this type in autumn 10 cm deep at 12 cm intervals; preferably in well-drained soil in sun. This tulip can stay outside, but do cover it with leaf mould.

TULIPA Prinses Irene
Tulip - single, early

Flowering period: April.
Colour: orange.
Height: 20-30 cm.
There are many types of single, early tulips. Plant in October 8 cm deep at 10 cm intervals, in groups. This one has a strong stem making it suitable for borders. Light, lime rich soil in sun or partial shade. Winter hard.

Shrubs and conifers are the 'large plants' in your garden, and they play a large part in how your garden will finally look. In practice, however, you will usually group the smaller plants around the existing trees, shrubs and conifers in your garden which you do not wish to move. But it might be a good idea to think about the possibility of a radical change in your garden.

On the following pages are a number of shrubs and conifers which are easy to introduce into an existing garden.

These days you buy shrubs and conifers complete with their own clump of earth in a pot or net, both of which are quickly absorbed into the soil. Because of this they can be planted at any time during the year, but the best thing is to plant deciduous shrubs in winter (when they are not growing) and the evergreens in summer or spring (because they can dry out if planted in winter). Soak the root clump for a quarter of an hour in water and plant it in a hole which you then fill with good garden soil. If a shrub has buds on the old wood, just cut out the dead wood in winter: where a shrub has buds on the new branches you can prune quite heavily.

ACER palmatum 'Dissectum' atropurpureum
Maple
Flowering period: irrelevant.
Colour: red leaf in autumn.
Height: maximum 1 1/2 m by 2-3 m wide.
A very beautiful and decorative maple. A sheltered spot is necessary. It prefers acid soil and will take partial shade. Suitable shrub for rock and roof gardens.

AMELANCHIER lamarckii
Juneberry

Flowering period: April to May.
Colour: white (bloom), red (leaf).
Height: 3-5 m.
Demands little in the way of good soil, sun or moisture. In spring it is covered in white blossom; in autumn with lovely orange-red leaves. A beautiful shrub, that needs a fair amount of space as it broadens out.

AZALEA japonica
Japanese Azalea

Flowering period: April to May.
Colour: red, lilac, pink, white, orange-red.
Height: 60-120 cm.
Japanese azalea stays half or fully green. It needs full sun and acid, moist soil. Protect the shrub against cold wind, although most types are winter hardy.

AZALEA (knaphill-exbury)
Azalea

Flowering period: late May to June.
Colour: white, yellow, pink, orange, red.
Height: about 150 cm.
This azalea must have moist, fertile and lime free soil in light shade. Propagation is mainly by rooting cuttings. The flowers have a lovely scent and must be cut off as they die.

AZALEA mollis
Azalea

Flowering period: May to June.
Colour: pink, red, orange, yellow.
Height: 100-200 cm.
Plant in moist, well-drained, fertile and lime rich soil in light shade. Break off full blown flowers immediately. In autumn the leaves take on lovely tints.

BERBERIS ottawensis 'Superba'
Barberry
Flowering period: April to May.
Colour: yellow, red.
Height: up to 2 m.
A strong shrub that likes sun and not too damp soil. Loses its russet leaves in winter. Propagate by rooting cuttings in summer. Very good in groups and beds needing colour contrast.

BERBERIS thunbergii 'Atro-purpurea'
Barberry
Flowering period: –
Colour: green; red in autumn.
Height: 75-100 cm.
Needs not too damp soil and full sun. It grows quickly and is often used for hedges (3 per meter) or as a filler around slower growing trees and shrubs.

CEDRUS atlantica 'Glauca'
Atlas Cedar

Flowering period: –
Colour: blue-white needles.
Height: 4-6 m; according to age up to 20 m.
Thrives in dry, well-drained, lime rich soil. A spot out of the wind is desirable. With its unpredictable growth it should stand alone, e.g. on a lawn.

CHAENOMELES superba
Japanese Quince

Flowering period: March to April.
Colour: flame red.
Height: 2 m.
The dwarf quince needs little goodness from the soil, but must have full sun and shelter from the north wind. Prune occasionally for good, regular flowering. Suitable for walls, rough hedges and to stand alone.

CHAMAECYPARIS laws.
'Columnaris Glauca'
Lawson Cypress
Flowering period: –
Colour: bluish green.
Height: 3-7 m.
The cypress flourishes in all soils, as long as sufficiently damp. It grows slowly into a lovely pillar shape. Plant in large gardens in groups. This cypress will not withstand sea winds.

CHAMAECYPARIS pisifera
'Plumosa Aurea'
Sawara Cypress
Flowering period: –
Colour: gold-green, bronze-yellow.
Height: 3-4 m.
Needs moist, humus rich soil in partial shade. Will not withstand too much heat and dryness, and needs shelter from sea winds. Suitable for small gardens, in groups in rock gardens or mixed in beds. Propagate from cuttings or seeds.

CLEMATIS 'Mad.le Coultre'
Clematis

Flowering period: June to August.
Colour: white.
Height: 2-3 m (climber).
Needs moist, loamy soil. Do not plant flush with walls; leave some space. After flowering, prune away half the length. Protect the base of the clematis from sun.

CORNUS alba 'Elegantissima'
Dogwood

Flowering period: –
Colour: green with silver edges; red in autumn.
Height: about 2 m.
Thrives in not too damp soil in a sunny spot. To obtain a good winter colour, prune well late March. Propagate by rooting cuttings in summer.

CORNUS alba 'Sibirica'
Dogwood

Flowering period: –
Colour: coral (winter bark).
Height: about 2 m.
Grows in both moist and dry soil. Will take shade but prefers warmer soil in a sunny spot. Plant close together in groups to make the most of the winter colour.

COTONEASTER watereri
'Pendulus'
Cotoneaster
Flowering period: May to June.
Colour: white (bloom), red (berry).
Height: 60 cm.
This evergreen demands little from the soil. Plant it complete with the earth around its roots. It is tough and quick growing; often with unequal growth. A good soil coverer. Sometimes tied up during growth.

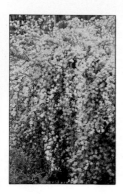

CYTISUS praecox 'Allgold'
Broom

Flowering period: May to June.
Colour: yellow.
Height: 0.5-2 m.
Often grown in poor, sandy soil, it also does well in other types of earth, with the exception of acid or lime. Its seed is very durable and therefore also good for propagation. Will not withstand severe frosts.

DEUTZIA gracilis
Deutzia

Flowering period: May to June.
Colour: white.
Height: up to 200 cm.
An elegant shrub that thrives in heavy, fertile soil. Every two years cut back old, heavy branches to ground level. Could be sensitive to late spring frosts. Propagate from cuttings in June-July.

ERICA carnea
Heather

Flowering period: between November and March, depending on type.
Colour: pink, red, white.
Height: 15-35 cm.
Prefers rather light, humus rich, acid soil, with sufficient moisture. Will also grow in lime. Blooms best in full sun. Propagate on a small scale by bending long shoots to ground and covering with soil to root.

FORSYTHIA intermedia 'Lynwood'
Forsythia
Flowering period: April to May.
Colour: golden yellow.
Height: 2-3 m.
Plant in well-drained, fertile soil with lime in a warm and sunny spot. Right after flowering, cut back to a few centimetres along the old wood. Allow young shoots to grow. Propagate by rooting cuttings (in winter these must be 20 cm long).

GINKGO ßiloba
Maidenhair Tree

Flowering period: –
Colour: yellow (fruit); yellow leaf in autumn.
Height: 20-30 m; 4-6 m in first 10-15 years.
A very old tree from China. Very attractive all year, even though it seldom forms fruit in this part of the world. It must be planted in fairly dry to moist soil which can contain lime.

HIBISCUS syriacus 'Wood-bridge'
Hibiscus
Flowering period: late July to October.
Colour: pale red.
Height: 2 m.
Needs well-drained, rather rich soil in a sunny and sheltered spot. If necessary, it can be well pruned each year in April. Young plants will not withstand severe weather, but older shrubs are fairly winter hard.

HYDRANGEA macrophylla
Common Hydrangea

Flowering period: August to
September.
Colour: white, pink, red, blue.
Height: 100-180 cm.
Grows best in slightly moist, lime
rich soil in shade. Cut away dead
wood. The hardy ones are winter
hardy. Encourage growth by
spraying with solution of iron
sulphate in water (10 g to
5 litres).

JUNIPERUS chinensis
'Plumosa Aurea'
Juniper
Flowering period: –
Colour: golden yellow, yellow-
green.
Height: 0.8-1 m; older bushes
to 2 m.
Demands little from the soil, but
does not like fierce sun. This one
grows very wide and in layers.
Take this into account when
planting. Take cuttings for rooting.

JUNIPERUS virginiana
'Skyrocket'
Pencil Cedar
Flowering period: –
Colour: blue-green.
Height: 10-15 years 3-4 m;
then 6-8 m.
This juniper thrives in dry, slightly
acid soil with lime. It is pillar-
shaped and can be planted in
groups or alone. Take cuttings for
rooting.

LABURNUM watereri 'Vossii'
Golden Chain

Flowering period: late May.
Colour: golden yellow.
Height: up to 8-10 m.
Grows in all not too damp soils,
even dry, sandy earth. Prefers a
warm, sunny spot. Do not leave
the seeds on the tree too long.
Root cuttings in winter. Cut the
woody spring shoots at an acute
angle to 20 cm long.

LONICERA periclymenum
'Serotina'
Honeysuckle
Flowering period: July to
October.
Colour: pink, white (bloom);
red (berry).
Height: 250-300 cm (climb-
er).
Very easy to grow in any soil. Does
well in sun or shade, and can
therefore be planted under things
Take cuttings in September or
October in sheltered nursery-bed.

MAGNOLIA lilliiflora 'Nigra'
Magnolia

Flowering period: April to
May.
Colour: flame (inner); purple-
red (outer).
Height: up to 3 m.
Grows in humus rich, fertile soil,
but heavy clay can be used. Earth
must be fairly moist but not too
damp. Needs a sunny, sheltered
spot. Propagation should be left to
specialists.

MALUS moerlandsii 'Nico-line'
Crab Apple
Flowering period: May.
Colour: red; pale red fruit.
Height: 4-6 m.
Prefers deeply dug, well-drained soil and a good space in the sun. Pruning can be limited to the cutting out of unwanted branches in winter. Because of the width of the crown, groups must be planted well apart.

PASSIFLORA caerulea
Passion Flower

Flowering period: summer and autumn.
Colour: greenish white.
Height: 2-3 m (climber).
Passion flower is a sparse climber that likes light. From May to October it can stand outside somewhere sunny and sheltered. In winter, keep it inside, eventually in a cold green house. Water well during growth. Fertilise in summer.

PICEA abies 'Pygmaea'
Spruce

Flowering period: –
Colour: fresh green.
Height: 100 cm.
This spruce needs slightly moist, fertile soil. A very slow grower, it is particularly suitable for rock or roof garden. It forms very tight bushes.

PICEA glauca 'Conica'
Canadian Spruce

Flowering period: –
Colour: bluish green.
Height: 1-2 m.
This conical spruce grows very slowly and prefers a light, moist, well-drained, acid soil. Suitable for small or heather gardens, but should not be planted at the front because of its rather stiff shape.

PINUS mugo var.mughus
Mountain Pine

Flowering period: irrelevant.
Colour: dark green.
Height: up to 80 cm.
This grows in soil with lime or in peat. The earth should be slightly moist. This dwarf variety does best in rock and heather gardens and can also be grown in a roof garden.

PINUS nigra var. 'Austriaca'
Austrian Pine

Flowering period: –
Colour: dark green.
Height: 10-15 years 3-5 m; then to 30 m.
Demands almost nothing from the soil, but prefers sandy, lime rich earth. Values warmth, especially during growth. An outstanding tree for park and garden, also grown in dunes.

PRUNUS cistena
Cherry Plum

Flowering period: late March to early April.
Colour: pink (bloom); dark red (leaf).
Height: 5-7 m.
The prunus loves soil with lime and a sunny spot. This type is suitable for the garden and as a hedging plant. It goes well with the forsythia which has the same flowering period.

PRUNUS triloba
Ornamental Almond

Flowering period: late May.
Colour: pink.
Height: 2-3 m.
This variety has one of spring's most beautiful blossoms. It can also be planted it with sandy soil. Right after flowering prune the shoots. More shoots 30-60 cm long will then appear for the following year. A tree much used against walls.

PYRACANTHA 'Orange Glow'
Firethorn
Flowering period: June.
Colour: berries fade from deep red to deep orange.
Height: 2-3 m.
Can be planted in any soil, and flourishes in sun or shade. Planted against a wall, however, most berries will appear on the side facing the sun. Set it 20 cm from the wall. Stretch threads along the wall (raffia, for example).

RHODODENDRON hybride
Rhododendron

Flowering period: April to May.
Colour: pink, yellow, lilac, purple, red.
Height: 2-3 m.
Prefers a lightly shaded spot in moist, fertile and lime free soil. Protect from frosts and drying winds. Remove full blown flowers as soon as possible. Pruning is not usually necessary.

ROSA grandiflora
Rose

Flowering period: mainly June to July.
Colour: very varied.
Height: 60-110 cm.
Rose bush roots must not dry out. At least plant it with wet roots. Plant the root core 3 cm under the soil. These large flowered bush roses should be 40-50 cm from each other. Cut off full blown flowers.

ROSA floribunda
Rose

Flowering period: mainly June to July.
Colour: very varied.
Height: 35-125 cm.
Roses prefer an open, sunny spot. The soil must not be acid, too dry or too wet. Never plant roses where other roses have previously grown. This rose is often grown in a geometric pattern.

SPIRAEA bumalda 'Anthony Waterer'
Spiraea
Flowering period: July to September.
Colour: rose red (flower); the leaf later turns red.
Height: 80 cm.
Makes no special demands on the soil, but a place in the full sun is necessary. This sort should be cut back completely every year. Cuttings can be taken for rooting in summer.

SYMPHORICARPOS albus 'White Hedge'
Snowberry
Flowering period: June to September.
Colour: reddish white (bloom); white (berry).
Height: 2 m.
Grows in sun or shade in very poor soil. Propagate by rooting cuttings in winter: cut woody stems to 25 cm and put in the ground to 3/4 of their length. Suitable for roof or garden.

SYRINGA vulgaris
Lilac

Flowering period: May.
Colour: white, lilac-pink, mauve.
Height: up to 5-7 m.
Syringa needs good, preferably loamy, soil which must not be too moist. Give it lime once a year. It likes to stand in the sun. Limit pruning to removal of old wood. Full blown flowers should also be cut away.

TAXUS baccata 'Fastigiata Aureomarginata'
Yew
Flowering period: –
Colour: dark green; young shoots yellow to bright green.
Height: 10-15 years to 120 cm; then to 500 cm.
Taxus grows, rather slowly, in any moist soil, but preferably clay. Protect from heavy frosts with rush mats. Can be cut to any shape. Very suitable for hedges.

THUJA occidentalis
White Cedar

Flowering period: –
Colour: dark green.
Height: 10-15 years 2-3 m; then to 20 m.
Grows in any soil as long as it is well-drained. Can be shaped into a lovely, smooth hedge. It is an evergreen that can be propagated from cuttings or seeds.

WISTERIA sinensis
Wisteria

Flowering period: April to May.
Colour: blue, violet.
Height: up to 6 m.
Wisteria needs fertile, well-drained but moist soil in a warm, sunny spot. Propagate from the tendrils of plants with good flowers, or by grafting the roots. Use: covering for walls and pergolas (with support).

Originally all plants were wild, but those covered by this guide so far are mainly cultivated, refined through nursery growing: strong, disease resistant, excellent flowering plants with blooms in many shades.

In the past few years, however, there has been a growing interest in 'wild' plants. This does not mean that they necessarily come straight from a wood or meadow, but that they are available from nurseries in roughly the same form as they are found in the wild. The interest in these plants seems to coincide with an interest in our environment. And, of course, it is often thought that a garden with wild plants needs less attention, but this is only partly true. If you allow your garden to run wild, the strongest plants will take over. It is then a question of whether or not this improves the look of the garden. Naturally, the less a plant is cultivated, the easier it is to look after and the more at home it seems, but even a natural garden needs attention if you want to make it really pretty. Only then will you make the most of the special charm of these plants.

AJUGA reptans
Bugle

Flowering period: May to July.
Colour: blue, purple.
Height: 15-30 cm.
Flourishes in sun or partial shade. It grows quickly and must be kept in check. A good soil coverer. Take cuttings in autumn or spring; or sow seeds outside in April.

ALLIUM schoenoprasum
Chives

Flowering period: June to July.
Colour: pale lilac.
Height: 15-30 cm.
Plant in the sun in the kitchen border or along the edge of a bed. Propagate from seed or young bulbs in spring. Needs well-drained garden soil and full sun. Tastes good in salads, etc.

ARMERIA maritima
Thrift

Flowering period: May to June.
Colour: pink, pale pink, red, white.
Height: 10-20 cm.
Sow in spring in sandy soil, or take cuttings in autumn (or spring). Prefers well-drained soil and a sunny spot. Suitable for edges, in groups in beds or rock gardens.

ASPERULA odorata
Sweet Woodruff

Flowering period: June to July.
Colour: white, lilac-pink.
Height: 7-10 cm.
Prefers well-drained soil. Suitable for a sunny spot along edges or in the rock garden. Protect from heavy rain in winter. The dried leaves have a nice perfume.

ASTRANTIA major
Masterwort

Flowering period: June to July.
Colour: pink.
Height: 40-70 cm.
This is an easy to grow perennial that likes moist, humus rich soil in partial shade. A wild flower that grows mainly on mountains, it comes originally from the Pyrenees. Cuttings can be taken.

ATHYRIUM filix femina
Lady-Fern

Flowering period: –
Colour: light green.
Height: 30-80 cm.
Thrives in moist, humus rich soil in full or partial shade. Easy to propagate from cuttings. Good for filling in between low-growing spreading plants, or between trees and shrubs.

AVENA sempervirens
Wild Oat

Flowering period: June to July.
Colour: blue-green leaves and stalks; silver plumes.
Height: 100 cm.
This is a turf-like, evergreen. Plant in spring in well-drained soil in the sun. Cut back the old plants in spring.

BLECHNUM spicant
Hard-Fern

Flowering period: –
Colour: dark green.
Height: 10-40 cm.
Thrives in full or partial shade in moist soil. The evergreen leaves are leathery. Grows wild here along ditches and embankments in sandy soil. Cuttings can be taken.

CALTHA palustris
King Cup

Flowering period: March to July.
Colour: yellow.
Height: 10-20 cm.
A very common wild flower which grows along banks. In a garden it will only grow in moist, humus rich soil in partial shade. It propagates itself from seed, but cuttings can be taken as long as the roots are kept damp.

CATANANCHE caerulea
Cupid's Dart

Flowering period: June to
August.
Colour: purple, white.
Height: 60-90 cm.
Plant out in spring in loose, well-
drained soil in the sun. Propagate
by dividing roots in late summer.
Prune old plants in spring. Good
dried flower (hang upside down to
dry).

CORTADERIA selloana
Pampas Grass

Flowering period: August to
October.
Colour: silver plumes; bluish
leaves.
Height: 45-90 cm.
Must be planted in March-April in
well-drained soil in a sunny spot.
Take cuttings in April. A dose of
fertiliser is advisable during
growth.

CORYDALIS lutea
Yellow Fumitory

Flowering period: May to
September.
Colour: yellow.
Height: 25 cm.
A perennial much grown in France
and Italy, but one which grows
well here in moist soil with humus
in shade. Easy to grow, it propagates itself readily from seeds.
Nice to mix with ferns and
decorative grasses.

DESCHAMPSIA caespitosa
Tufted Hair-Grass

Flowering period: June to
August.
Colour: green.
Height: 80 cm.
Thrives in moist, humus rich soil.
It grows in woods and marshland.
Much used in dried bouquets, as
long as it is picked and dried
properly.

DRYAS octopetala
Mountain Avens

Flowering period: May to
June.
Colour: white with yellow.
Height: 10 cm.
A common plant with a short
flowering period; but it is a fine
soil covering. Needs a sunny spot
in dry, well-drained, lime rich
earth. The top soil must be loose.
Divide for propagation in spring.

ECHINOPS ritro
Globe Thistle

Flowering period: July to
August.
Colour: steel blue.
Height: 90 cm.
Plant spring or autumn in ordinary
garden soil in sun or light shade.
Propagate from cuttings or
dividing the roots. Worth growing
for its lovely flower.

EPILOBIUM angustifolium
Willow herb

Flowering period: July to October.
Colour: pink.
Height: 80-100 cm.
A common wild flower. There is also a fully- and a half-cultured variety. The one here is the wild fireweed. Plant it in dry, sandy soil, preferably in a wood, or in sandy soil near water.

ERYNGIUM
Eryngium

Flowering period: July to August.
Colour: steel blue, grey-blue.
Height: 45-60 cm.
Grows in rather dry soil in full sun. Propagate by dividing the roots in autumn. Or cuttings can be taken spring and autumn. A decorative plant, but do not allow it too much moisture in winter.

FESTUCA glauca
Fescue

Flowering period: May to July.
Colour: purple, silvery.
Height: 25 cm.
This forms thick clumps and is very suitable for borders. Plant in ordinary soil in full sun. Propagate by dividing the clumps or from seed sown early spring.

FRAGARIA vesca
Wild Strawberry

Flowering period: May to September.
Colour: white (flower); red (fruit).
Height: 10-20 cm.
The wild strawberry spreads quickly. It grows wild between wood and grass. Both flower and fruit (edible) are pretty, so this wild plant, with no special needs, is a nice addition to a natural garden.

GLYCERIA maxima 'Variegata'
Reed-Grass

Flowering period: July to August.
Colour: yellow-white stripe.
Height: 100-200 cm.
One of the few ornamental grasses that needs a moist, peaty soil. Propagate by dividing in April-May. Suitable for planting at the edge of ponds.

HERACLEUM mantegaz-
zianum
Hogweed
Flowering period: June to August.
Colour: white.
Height: 150-250 cm.
Hogweed is a decorative plant, both fresh and dried. It needs sun or partial shade beside water or at the back of a bed, and ordinary soil. Propagate by dividing or from seed in autumn.

HESPERIS matronalis
Damask Violet

Flowering period: May to July.
Colour: white, pink, with evening perfume.
Height: 60-90 cm.
Grows in ordinary soil in full sun, but water regularly. Plant out in spring or autumn. Fertilise in May. Propagate by dividing the full grown plants in spring or autumn.

HIERACIUM aurantiacum
Hawk Weed

Flowering period: June to August.
Colour: bright yellow, orange.
Height: 30 cm.
Grows in poor soil in the sun, but must have good drainage. Propagate by dividing or from seed. Suitable for rock, heather or natural gardens.

HOLCUS lanatus 'Variegatus'
Yorkshire Fog

Flowering period: June to August.
Colour: green; white plumes.
Height: 30-90 cm.
Demands virtually nothing from the soil, except not too much moisture. It is a perennial grass which forms strong clumps.

KOELERIA glauca
Hair-Grass

Flowering period: June to September.
Colour: cream-white, bluish.
Height: up to 30 cm.
Hair-grass must be planted in spring in the sun. It likes sandy soil. Propagate by dividing or from seed in spring.

LAMIUM maculatum 'Varlegatum'
Spotted Dead-Nettle
Flowering period: May to August.
Colour: pink.
Height: 15-25 cm.
A common wild plant; everyone knows the white variety. To cultivate there is a yellow and a pink and this one, the 'variegatum', also has an interesting leaf. The plant needs moist, humus rich soil and shade.

LUZULA nivea
Woodrush

Flowering period: July to August.
Colour: green; white flower.
Height: 30-60 cm.
Prefers not too fertile but moist soil. The leaves stay green in winter. Propagate by dividing or from seed. Very good for mixing with ferns.

LYSIMACHIA nummularia
Creeping Jenny

Flowering period: May to
July.
Colour: yellow.
Height: about 10 cm.
Grows in fertile soil (one part leaf
mould, one part sand). Some
shade is a good idea. Much used
as a soil cover. Propagate by
dividing in spring or autumn. Very
good for natural gardens,
especially in damp spots.

LYTHRUM salicaria
Purple Loosestrife

Flowering period: June to
August.
Colour: purple.
Height: 70 cm.
Ideal for the edges of ponds or
brooks, but it will also do well in a
bed. Propagate by dividing in April
or October. A common wild plant,
and one of the prettiest for
watersides.

MATTEUCIA struthiopteris
Ostrich Feather Fern

Flowering period: –
Colour: light green.
Height: 60-80 cm.
Prefers moist, humus rich, acid
soil in shade. Propagate by
dividing. Plant in May at 60 cm
intervals. In autumn the leaves
turn yellow and die off.

MISCANTHUS sinensis
'Zebrinus'
Miscanthus
Flowering period: July to
October.
Colour: white plumes.
Height: 125 cm.
Plant in March-April in ordinary
soil in the sun. Propagation can be
done by dividing in the spring. The
cuttings should not be too small or
they will not take.

MOLINIA caerulea
Moor-Grass

Flowering period: August to
September.
Colour: green.
Height: 50 cm.
Grows best in poor, rough soil.
Never use fertiliser. A perennial
grass, providing its environment is
not altered.

ORIGANUM vulgare
Marjoram

Flowering period: June to
August.
Colour: purple.
Height: 30-50 cm.
Marjoram likes well-drained, lime
rich soil and a sunny spot. Sow
out under glass April-May in
sandy soil. Take cuttings in
spring. Can be used in cooking.

OSMUNDA regalis
Royal Fern

Flowering period: –
Colour: yellow-green.
Height: 50-150 cm.
Needs a somewhat shaded, but not too dark spot. The soil must be moist and lime rich. Plant between shrubs or mixed with woodland flowers. Propagate by dividing the root stock.

PENNISETUM
Pennisetum, Fountain Grass
Flowering period: August to October.
Colour: purplish plumes.
Height: 60-80 cm.
Grows well in ordinary soil which must have good drainage, in a sunny spot. Protect in winter. Can be transplanted, and propagated by dividing in April.

PHALARIS arundinacea
Reed-Grass

Flowering period: –
Colour: green.
Height: 60-100 cm.
Plant in a sunny but moist spot. This perennial shows to advantage by ponds or in beds. Propagate by dividing. In summer it has large green to purplish plumes.

PHYLLITIS scolopendrium
Hart's-tongue Fern

Flowering period: –
Colour: dark green.
Height: 20-30 cm.
This fern is an evergreen. It needs lime or humus rich soil, preferably in a moist spot. For example, against a damp wall. Suitable for dry stone walls and wall troughs.

POLYGONUM bistorta
Snakeweed

Flowering period: May to June.
Colour: pale pink.
Height: 60 cm.
Grows in both sun and partial shade. Prefers fertile, moist soil. Plant in spring or autumn. Propagate by dividing. In this country the plant grows wild in woods and in marshy fields.

POLYPODIUM vulgare
Polypody

Flowering period: –
Colour: green.
Height: 30 cm.
A wild fern that prefers acid, humus rich soil in shade. Propagate by dividing root stock, but it grows rather slowly.

PRIMULA veris
Cowslip

Flowering period: March to April.
Colour: pale to dark yellow.
Height: 15-30 cm.
Cowslips need fertile soil in slight shade, and grow so strongly that they can be split every year. In the wild they grow in marshy meadows and are used in cross-breeding with cultivated plants.

STACHYS palustris
Marsh Woundwort

Flowering period: June to September.
Colour: lilac with white.
Height: 60-100 cm.
In the wild this marsh plant is often found along river banks. Now, with the increasing interest in wild plants, it is often found in nurseries. Even so, it still needs little more than moist, sandy soil and some sun.

SYMPHYTUM grandiflorum
Comfrey

Flowering period: May to June.
Colour: white, pink, purple, yellow.
Height: 60-120 cm.
Comfrey needs moist soil in sun or partial shade. It is very nice when left to run wild. Plant in spring or autumn. Propagate by seed in the same seasons.

THYMUS vulgaris
Thyme

Flowering period: May to July.
Colour: lilac.
Height: 25 cm.
Needs well-drained soil and sun. Mainly grown in rock or herb gardens. Sow or plant in spring. After flowering, pinch out tops for a bushier plant. This is a kitchen herb.

VALERIANA officinalis
Valerian

Flowering period: July to September.
Colour: pale pink.
Height: up to 125 cm.
Only grows in moist, marshy soil, such as along water banks. The pharmaceutical industry uses the root stocks for valerian tincture.

VERONICA filiformis
Speedwell

Flowering period: May to June.
Colour: pale blue with white.
Height: 10 cm.
Plant in spring or autumn in ordinary, not too dry soil in sun or light shade. Propagate by dividing in spring or autumn. The thin, thread-like stems root easily, quickly forming thick clumps. Good substitute for grass.

Even though the cut flower is not a separate variety, it has its own section, because when you plan your garden you will take into account the fact that a number of plants make good cut flowers. In this chapter we treat nine of them. But do remember: not all plants with masses of blooms belong to this section, since there are flowers that wilt quickly if they are cut.

The following plants give good cut flowers: Marigold, Carnation, Aster, Chinese Carnation, Clarkia, Cosmea, Dahlia, Scabious, Phlox, Fleabane, Marguerite, Goat's Beard, Baby's Breath, Gladiolus, Pot Marigold, Iris, Love-in-a-mist, Musk Mallow, Amaranthus, Poppy, Blanket Flower, Cornflower, Lathyrus, Daffodil, Nasturtium, Lankspur, Rose, Salvia, Solomon's Seal, Syringa, Spiraea, Tulip, Stock, Lady's Mantle, Red Hot Poker, Zinnia, Azalea, Sunflower, Heliopsis and Cornflower.

Cut the flowers in the morning or evening and put them in a bucket of water so they can soak up plenty of moisture, with the exception of Lathyrus, which needs only a tiny amount of water.

ASTER alpinus
Michaelmas Daisy

Flowering period: May to June.
Colour: mauve, purple, white, with yellow centre.
Height: 10-20 cm.
Naturally all the asters are outstanding cut flowers. We give here a low growing type that gives masses of blooms for little care. Cut the flowers when half or fully open.

CHRYSANTHEMUM maximum
Giant Marguerite

Flowering period: June to October.
Colour: white; sometimes artificially coloured.
Height: 40-80 cm.
One of the best cut flowers; countless new shapes and colours are being developed in greenhouses. But look twice at the pink, yellow or blue marguerites; you will then see that they are artificially coloured!

DAHLIA
Dahlia

Flowering period: July to October.
Colour: red, yellow, white, orange; in many mixtures.
Height: 50-90 cm.
Its many varieties provide a good selection of cutting flowers. Often grown apart specially for cutting, bedding dahlia blooms can also be cut now and then. A mass of flowers for little attention.

DIANTHUS
Carnation

Flowering period: June to August.
Colour: white, yellow, pink, red.
Height: 30-60 cm.
Like the aster and rose, the carnation is much cultivated for its flowers. Those grown specially for cutting need lots of attention; better to leave these to a nursery. But there is still a wide choice for the garden.

LATHYRUS latifolius
Sweet Pea

Flowering period: June to September.
Colour: mauve, pink, white, blue.
Height: to 200 cm (climber).
Grown for the fresh colours of their flowers and, in some cases, the wonderful scent. Those shown here have no scent; for this choose 'odoratus'. As well as being a fine cut flower, it is also a good climber.

LUPINUS russell
Lupin

Flowering period: May to July; September.
Colour: blue, red, pink, yellow, etc.
Height: 80-100 cm.
Mainly grown as bedding plants or to improve the soil, lupins are also fine cut flowers not least because of their huge range of colours. Easy to grow, they give a mass of blooms, even when used for cutting.

ROSA grandiflora
Rose

This rose is a great favourite for cutting. Grown all over the world for its beautiful flower, with countless colour variations. Roses need extra care, both to cultivate and to cut, but this just increases the pleasure for the grower.

SYRINGA vulgaris
Lilac

Flowering period: May to June.
Colour: purple, blue, white.
Height: to 5 meters.
Like the rose, a well known bush often grown for cutting. Frequently grown in a greenhouse to force the flowers for early sale. The flowering period of your garden syringa is, however, long enough to give much pleasure.

ZINNIA elegans
Zinnia

Flowering period: June to October.
Colour: red, pink, yellow, orange, white and mixtures.
Height: 15-100 cm.
There are many sturdy zinnias with lovely colours for cutting. The long flowering period means lots of blooms for the house. Cut flowers when outer petals are open but heart is still closed.

As with cut flowers, this is not a separate type, but even so we would point out that the flowers of a number of plants remain pretty when dried.

Those from seed include Baby's Breath, Love-in-a-mist, Poppy, Lankspur, Honesty and Wild Teasel.

Flowers which are naturally rather dry also belong to this group, the best known being: Acroclineum, Catananche, Helychrysum, Helipterum, Lonas Inodora, Rhodanthe, Statice.

From the perennials, the following can be dried: Yarrow, Everlasting Pearl, Echinops, Hydrangea and Chinese Lantern.

In addition, there are a number of decorative grasses and heathers which are suitable for drying and also some wild plants like Hogweed, Clematis and Fireweed.

Cut the flowers or fruit when they are just open or ripe and hang them upside down in bunches in a dry, well ventilated, dark place. Let the bunches dry for about two months. With some blooms you need to use dry flower powder to keep the colour sharp. When the flowers are completely dried, you can make a bouquet which will add colour to the darker spots in your home.

ACHILLEA filipendullna
Yarrow

Flowering period: June to August.
Colour: yellow.
Height: 80-100 cm.
One of the best known and most popular dried flowers, its lovely umbellate flowers are easy to dry. Cut when in full bloom and hang upside down in a dry place. Powder with alum for full colour retention.

ACROCLINEUM helipterum roseum
Immortelle
Flowering period: mid-June to August.
Colour: red, white, pink.
Height: 30-60 cm.
A lovely flower for a dried bouquet. This is the original dried flower. It is a bloom (and stem) which retains colour and sturdiness when dried. Cut the flowers and hang upside down to dry.

ANAPHALIS triplinervis
Everlasting Flower

Flowering period: June to October.
Colour: white-green.
Height: 20-40 cm.
This resembles the immortelle with the same 'paper-like' quality. Easy to grow, it is not bothered by dryness. Cut the blooms on a warm day and hang upside down in a dry place.

RTADERIA selloana
mpas Grass

wering period: September
October.
lour: silver plumes.
ight: 2-3 meters.
A ovely basis for a dried bouquet,
even though rather large.
Successful growing is dependent
well-drained, moist soil. Cut
es on a dry day and allow to
well before use.

CUCURBITA
Gourd

Flowering period: July.
Colour: yellow-white (bloom);
green, orange, yellow (fruit).
Height: creeps to 3.5 m.
The gourd can be edible, but it is
the inedible artificial gourd which
is most often grown in the garden
for its decorative fruit. This fruit
can be dried, and will retain its
beauty.

DELPHINIUM Ajacis
Larkspur

Flowering period: mid-June
to August.
Colour: pink, blue, purple.
Height: 30-60 cm.
Not a real drying flower: the colour
fades and the stem turns brown.
Even so, a nice bouquet can be
made which will last. This is also
true of other cut flowers: so
experimenting is a good idea.

ECHINOPS ritro
Globe Thistle

Flowering period: June to
August.
Colour: mauve-blue.
Height: 60-80 cm.
Very attractive for the garden with
its striking spherical bloom and
lovely silver-green leaf. After it has
served its decorative purpose
outside, the flowers can be cut and
used in bouquets, with or without
other blooms.

LUNARIA biennis
Honesty

Flowering period: June to
July.
Colour: mauve.
Height: 80-120 cm.
Honesty is a traditional dried
flower, or rather fruit because it is
the seed pods which are dried.
After the flowers, also pretty, tie up
the plant to prevent damage to the
brittle stems. When dried, remove
the outer ease.

STATICE limonium sinuatum
Sea Lavender

Flowering period: July to
October.
Colour: yellow, pink, mauve
and mixtures.
Height: 60-100 cm.
Pre-eminent amongst drying
flowers because of the colours
(and there are many) stay bright
when dried, particularly if
powdered with alum. Cut blooms
on a dry, sunny day and hang
upside down to dry.

INDEX

YELLOW FLOWERS

WHITE FLOWERS

BLUE FLOWERS

Aster 40, 83
Aubrieta 14
Bugle 75
Ceratostigma 17
Cornflower 16, 41
Curds Dart 77
Flax 48
Forget-me-not 28, 49
Gentian 21
Globe Thistle 77
Grape Hyacinth 63
Gromwell 26
Hound's Tongue 17
Hydrangea 71

Iris 24
Larkspur 17, 43
Lavender 25
Love-in-a-Mist 50
Monkshood 12
Primrose 30
Salvia 32
Scabious 33
Sicalcea 34
Sweet Pea 47
Trinity Flower 35
Verbena 55
Wisteria 73

ORANGE FLOWERS

African Marigold 54
Avens 21
Azalea 67, 68
Buttercup 65
Californian Poppy 44
Chinese Lantern 29, 51
Cinquefoil 30
Cockscomb 41
Crown Imperial 61
Dimorphoteca 44
Firethorn 73
Foxtail Lily 60
Freesia 60

Gazania 45
Ligularia 26
Lily 63
Marigold 54
Monkey Flower 27
Nasturtium 55
Nemesia 50
Peruvian Lily 12
Poppy 28
Portulaca 52
Red Hot Poker 25, 54
Siberian Wallflower 41
Tulip 65, 66

PURPLE FLOWERS

Aster 40, 83
Astilbe 14
Aubrieta 14, 39
Busy Lizzie 46
Columbine 13, 39
Cornflower 16
Crocus 59
Day Lily 23
Fleabane 20
Harlequin Flower 65
Heather 19
Iris 24, 62
Larkspur 17

Lilac 74
Lupin 26, 48, 49
Meadow Rue 35
Michaelmas Daisy 14
Mirabilis 49
Nemesia 50
Pansy 36, 55, 56
Pansy 55
Pasque Flower 31
Phlox 29, 51
Scarlet Pimpernel 38
Snake's Head 61
Tulip 65, 66

GROUND-COVERING PLANTS

Aubrieta   14, 39
Awl-leaved Pearlwort   32
Biting Stonecrop   33
Candytuft   23, 46
Chinese Aster   40
Cranesbill   21
Daisy   15, 39
Dryas   19
Edelweiss   25
Evening Primrose   28
Forget-me-not   28
Golden Alyssum   12, 38
Gromwell   26
Knotweed   30
Lesser Periwinkle   36

Lobelia   48
Matricaria   49
New Zealand Burr   11
Ornamental Strawberry   19
Portulaca   52
Rock Rose   22, 45
Rock-Cress   13
Sedum   33, 34
Self-Heal   31
Snapdragon (low)   39
Snow-in-Summer   16
Soapwort   32, 53
Stork's Bill   20
Sweet Violet   36
Sweet Woodruff   76

SHADE-LOVING PLANTS

Nearly all plants need sunlight for growing and flowering. Yet there are plants that prefer shade, under bushes or on a spot in your garden where the sun does not reach.
The plants mentioned below are not all shadeplants of this type, but all of them like half-shade, which means that they need only a few hours of sun a day. With these plants you can even make a garden facing north something beautiful!

Astilbe   14
Aubrieta   14
Bell Flower   15, 16
Cypress   69
Dead-Nettle   79
Dogwood   69
Glory of the Snow   59
Goat's Beard   13
Honeysuckle   71
Hydrangea   71
Leopard's Bane   19, 44
Lesser Periwinkle   36
Ligularia   26

Lily of the Vally   59
Lung-wort   31
Lysimachia   27
Monkshood   12
Pine   72
Plantain Lily   23
Primrose   31, 52
Rhododendron   73
Rock-Cress   13
Snakeweed   81
Snowdrop   61
Squill   65
Star of Bethlehem   64
Waldsteinia   36
Windflower   13
Winter Aconite   60

INDEX OF ENGLISH PLANT NAMES